Still Not Easy Being British:
Struggles for a Multicultural Citizenship

Still Not Easy Being British:
Struggles for a Multicultural Citizenship

Tariq Modood

Trentham Books
Stoke on Trent, UK and Sterling, USA

Trentham Books Limited
Westview House   22883 Quicksilver Drive
734 London Road   Sterling
Oakhill   VA 20166-2012
Stoke on Trent   USA
Staffordshire
England ST4 5NP

First published 2010

British Library Cataloguing-in-Publication Data
A catalogue record for this book is available from the
British Library

ISBN 978 1 85856 480 7

Designed and typeset by Trentham Books Ltd and printed in
Great Britain by Page Bros (Norwich) Ltd, Norfolk

For my sisters Jasmin and Ghizela,
with love

Books by Tariq Modood

Multiculturalism: A Civic Idea. Polity, 2007

Multicultural Politics: Racism, Ethnicity and Muslims in Britain. University of Minnesota Press and University of Edinburgh Press, 2005

Not Easy Being British: Colour, Culture and Citizenship. Runnymede Trust and Trentham Books, 1992

(with F Ahmad and S Lissenburgh) *South Asian Women and Employment in Britain: the Interaction of Gender and Ethnicity*. Policy Studies Institute, 2003

(with J Carter and S Fenton) *Ethnicity and Employment in Higher Education*. Policy Studies Institute, 1999

(with R Berthoud, J Lakey, J Nazroo, P Smith, S Virdee and S Beishon) *Ethnic Minorities in Britain: Diversity and Disadvantage; The Fourth National Survey of Ethnic Minorities*. Policy Studies Institute, 1997

(with H Metcalf and S Virdee) *Asian Self Employment: the interaction of culture and economics in England*. Policy Studies Institute, 1996

(with S Beishon and S Virdee) *Ethnic Minority Families*. Policy Studies Institute 1998

(with M Shiner) *Ethnic Minorities and Higher Education: Why Are There Differential Rates of Entry?*, Policy Studies Institute, 1994.

(with S Beishon and S Virdee) *Changing Ethnic Identities*. Policy Studies Institute, 1994

Edited Books

(with J Salt) *Migration and Citizenship: The UK Experience*. Palgrave, 2011 forthcoming

(with G Levey) *Secularism, Religion and Multicultural Citizenship* (Foreword by Charles Taylor). Cambridge University Press, 2009

(with GG Raymond) The Construction of Minority Identities in France and Britain. Palgrave McMillan, 2007

(with A Triandafyllidou and R Zapata-Barrero) (eds) *Multiculturalism, Muslims and Citizenship: A European Approach*. Routledge, 2006

(with G Loury and S Teles) *Ethnicity, Social Mobility and Public Policy in the US and UK*. Cambridge University Press, 2005

(with S May and J Squires) *Ethnicity, Nationalism and Minority Rights*. Cambridge University Press, 2004

(with T Acland) *Race and Higher Education*. Policy Studies Institute, 1998

Church, State and Religious Minorities. Policy Studies Institute, 1997

(with P Werbner) *The Politics of Multiculturalism in the New Europe*. Zed Books, 1997

(with P Werbner) *Debating Cultural Hybridities: Identities and the Politics of Anti-Racism*. Zed Books, 1997

(with D Boucher and J Connelly) *Philosophy, History and Civilisation: Essays on R G Collingwood*. University of Wales Press, 1995

Contents

Foreword
Robin Richardson

I n the early 1990s the headteacher of a primary school in central England was made aware that some of the younger pupils at his school were distressed by a pictorial display on one of the classroom walls. A is for apple, the display said, B is for ball, C is for cat, and so on through to Z – all entirely customary, traditional, dearly familiar, part of the wallpaper in every infant classroom in the land. The parents of the children who were distressed were from a conservative Muslim background in rural Pakistan and the image which distressed them was labelled P is for pig. The headteacher changed the image and the label, so that P was now for pencil instead.

Somehow, this tiny episode found its way into a national newspaper and the headteacher was vigorously ridiculed and abused. 'For too long,' said a ponderous satire in the *Sun* on 12 November 1992, 'we have been teaching English in a white, middle-class, racist, sexist fashion. If we want to encourage immigrants to assimilate into our society we must help them to learn our language. For this reason the Government has decided to introduce a new alphabet tailored to the needs of Muslim pupils.' It then announced the new alphabet:

A is for Ayatollah, B is for Baghdad, C is for Curry, D is for Djabella, E is for Emir, F is for Fatwa, G is for Gaddafi, H is for Hezbollah, I is for Intifada, J is for Jihad, K is for Khomeni, L is for Lebanon. M is for Mecca, N is for Naan. O is for Onion Bhaji, P is for Palestine, Q is for Q8 [Kuwait], R is for Rushdie, S is for Saddam, T is for Tehran, U is for United Arab Emirates, V is for Vindaloo, W is for West Bank, X is for Xenophobia, Y is for Yasser Arafat, Z is for Zionist Imperialist Aggressor Running Dogs of the Great Satan. (*The Sun*, 12 November 1992)

Almost exactly a year earlier, the word 'Islamophobia' had been used for the first time in a piece of writing by someone in Britain. (Slightly earlier uses of the word in English occurred in writings in the United States. The French word *islamophobie* had been in use since 1912.) The author was Tariq Modood, at that time an officer at the Commission for Racial Equality (CRE) and the occasion was a book review in *The Independent*, subsequently reprinted in Modood's compilation entitled *Not Easy Being British*, published by Trentham Books in 1992. In the review itself, as also at greater length in other chapters in the compilation, Modood challenged the prevailing consensus in Britain's race equality community – race equality councils, race equality officers and advisers in local government, the CRE itself – about the nature of racism. Race and religion are not wholly dissimilar categories, he argued, and it is frequently impossible to disentangle discrimination based on race from discrimination based on religion or belief. He popularised the understanding that racism has two principal ingredients, to do respectively with colour and culture. He argued further that there needs in consequence to be a re-examination of the nature of Britishness, of the place of religious language and symbols in public life, of majority/ minority relationships, and of concepts of recognition and identity. Such considerations may seem a far cry from the practicalities of wall displays in primary schools. They are deeply relevant to the field of education, however, as also to other areas of society, and can illuminate the day-to-day options, choices and priorities of, amongst others, head-teachers and teachers.

Amongst individuals, the importance of *Not Easy Being British* was recognised and promoted through word-of-mouth recommendations and it became an underground classic. Its significance was also increasingly recognised in academia. Amongst policy-makers, however, and in the race equality community, its arguments were largely ignored. Anti-racists had been silent about cultural racism during *The Satanic Verses* affair in the late 1980s and continued silent on this topic through the coming years as well. Key events over the years would in due course include the Runnymede Trust report on Islamophobia in 1997 and its follow-up in 2004; the establishment of the Muslim Council of Britain in 1997; the media distortions and lies about *The Future of Multi-Ethnic Britain* (the Parekh Report) in 2000; the disturbances in northern cities in 2001 and the ensuing community cohesion agenda; the attacks in the United States, also 2001, and the ensuing invasions of Afghanistan and Iraq; the London bombs in 2005 and ensuing programmes to prevent violent extremism; attacks from left-leaning intellectuals from about 2004 onwards on multiculturalism, together with the allegation that Britain was 'sleep-walking towards segregation'; the Danish caricatures episode in 2007; frequent untrue stories in the media about, in a re-curring phrase, political correctness gone mad, blaming Muslims for threatening traditional British values; moral panics relating to the wear-ing of Islamic dress in public places; the media distortions of a modest proposal by the Archbishop of Canterbury to the effect that aspects of Islamic law should be formally recognised within UK law; Europe-wide demonising of Islam by far-right political parties, claiming that Europe and Islam have nothing in common, and the increasing support for these parties at local and national elections; media and government attacks on the Muslim Council of Britain throughout most of the decade after 2001; and the full adoption into UK equalities legislation, towards the end of the decade, of the discrete category of 'religion or belief'.

On these and other such events and trends, Tariq Modood has con-tinued to contribute to public debates. Partly, and invaluably, his contri-butions have been in academic books, articles and lectures, and through the activities of the Centre for the Study of Ethnicity and Citizenship at the University of Bristol, of which he is the founding director. Also, and equally invaluably, he has contributed through newspaper articles and the blogoshere, and through frequent appearances on radio and tele-vision. This volume contains a selection of these relatively non-specialist pieces.

In the satire cited above, the *Sun* was playing on fears about what it saw as the increasing influence of Islam in Britain and in the wider world. In doing this, it set out the default position, so to speak, held by non-Muslims about Muslims – the 'common sense' that is widely assumed unless a conscious effort is made to question it and to replace it. Six of the most frequent elements in the default position are these: a) Muslims are all much the same as each other, regardless of their ethnicity, nationality, social class, geographical location and political outlook, and regardless of how observant and religiously-oriented they are, or are not; b) the single most important thing about a 'Muslim' is that he

or she has certain religious beliefs and engages in certain religious practices, and accordingly everything a Muslim does is motivated by
religion; c) Muslims are totally other – they have few or no interests,
characteristics, needs, concerns or aspirations in common with non-
Muslims, and therefore the values of Muslims and non-Muslims are
incompatible with each other; d) Muslims are culturally, intellectually,
politically and morally inferior to non-Muslims – quick to take offence,
prone to irrationality and violence, hypocritical in the practice of their
religion – and in consequence do not possess any relevant and valuable
insights, perspectives and achievements from which non-Muslims may
learn and benefit; e) Muslims are a threat to non-Muslims – globally,
they may attack non-Muslim countries, as on 9/11, and are a threat to
the existence of Israel, and within non-Muslim countries they are a
treacherous and disloyal fifth column or enemy within; f) as a
consequence of the previous five perceptions, there is no possibility of
cooperation and partnership between 'them' and 'us', Muslims and
non-Muslims, working as equals on tasks which require mediation,
negotiation, compromise and partnership.

The *Sun* combined its attack on Islam with an attack on a particular
non-Muslim individual, a primary school headteacher who did not
understand, in the paper's view, the grave threats that Islam poses for
British society and how weak, vulnerable and unsure of itself Britain has
become. If even primary school headteachers do not grasp the serious-
ness of the situation we're all in, the *Sun* appeared to be saying, what
hope is there for the rest of us? Frequently it happens that moral panics
about Muslims in the modern media are combined in this way with
panics about the competence and reliability of non-Muslim authority
figures, for example headteachers, and non-Muslim administrators and
politicians. The effect may be to intimidate and demoralise them, and
to undermine their confidence. The writings of Tariq Modood can help
to stiffen their resolve, however, and help them to keep their heads and
their hearts at difficult times.

Anxieties about the competence and reliability of non-Muslim
authority figures have their origins in widespread social change, not
primarily or essentially in multiculturalism, and certainly not in Islam.
The problem is not in the first instance to do with differences of culture,
religion, ideology or civilisation. Rather, it is to do with conflicts of

material interest. Globally, the key conflicts are around power, influence, territory and resources, particularly oil. Within urban areas in Europe they are around employment, housing, health and education. Such conflicts between and within countries become 'religionised' or 'culturalised' – each side celebrates and idealises its own traditions and cultural heritage, including religion, and disparages and demonises the traditions of the other. Further, and even more importantly, the attacks in America on 9/11 were a vivid reminder that the governments of nation states – even of extremely powerful nation states – are no longer able to guarantee the security of their citizens. At the same time they cannot control, to the extent they did in the past, economic, cultural and ecological borders. The resulting insecurities lead to scapegoating and moral panics, with Muslims and other minorities as convenient enemies and targets, but not as the principal causes. Similarly authority figures such as primary school headteachers are convenient targets and scapegoats, not the real culprits. Keeping such things in mind can help maintain a sense of proportion.

In the coming years, as the Equality Act 2010 takes effect in Britain, there will be increasing awareness of 'religion or belief' as a protected characteristic in the new legislation. In this connection too, clear thinking and a robust sense of proportion will be vital. 'The law will protect the believer,' observed the Equality and Human Rights Commission in its briefings for the Equality Bill committee stages in the House of Lords in 2009, 'not the belief.' But as Tariq Modood shows at length in this book, religion is not only a belief system, something that an individual chooses to adopt or to reject. It is also a broad cultural tradition, something that an individual is born into and on the basis of which they may be discriminated against, or be the target of a hate crime, regardless of whether they are believers. In relation to challenging hostility and discrimination on grounds of religion, the latter understanding of religion is frequently the more relevant. This is well known in Northern Ireland, for example, and in many other parts of the world, including the Balkans, Lebanon, Nigeria and South Asia.

A key concept in equalities legislation is that of reasonable accommodation. At all times and in all places human beings make adjustments to their practices, customs and policies in order to accommodate a range of interests, needs and concerns. They typically do this through processes of discussion, dialogue, negotiation and compromise – namely by saying, in the words of the Hebrew scriptures, 'come now, let us reason together'. They engage with each other, that is to say, in a spirit of good will rather than with the use or threats of coercion and brute power. The root syllable of the word accommodation appears also in 'moderate' and 'modest' – the concern is to devise systems that are *good enough*, not totally perfect, and not making a great fuss or drawing attention to themselves.

In the preface written for Tariq Modood's 1992 compilation there was a quotation from a then recent article by the journalist Peregrine Worsthorne. He had claimed Islam was 'once a great civilisation worthy of being argued with' but had now 'degenerated into a primitive enemy fit only to be sensitively subjugated' (*Sunday Telegraph*, 3 February 1991). It is interesting that Worsthorne made two distinctions in this claim, the one to do with perception ('great civilisation'/'primitive enemy') and the other to do with forms of thinking and relating ('argued with'/'subjugated'.)

To see an individual or a group or a civilisation as 'worthy of being argued with' is necessarily to be open-minded towards them. The hall-marks of open-mindedness include readiness to change one's views, both of others and of oneself, in the light of new facts and evidence; not deliberately distorting, or recklessly over-simplifying, incontestable facts; not caricaturing the views of people with whom one disagrees; not over-generalising; not using double standards when comparing and contrasting others with oneself; seeing difference and disagree-ment as a resource for understanding more about oneself, not as a threat; seeking to understand other people's views and standpoints in their own terms, and recognising where they are coming from – the narratives and stories with which they interpret events; not claiming greater certainty than is warranted; and seeking consensus or, at least, a *modus vivendi* which keeps channels of communication open and permits all to maintain dignity.

These features of the open mind characterise, and indeed distinguish, the writings of Tariq Modood. They are also likely to be strengthened and emboldened amongst all those who read him.

Robin Richardson
May 2010

Introduction:
Britishness, Multiculturalism and Muslims

Much has changed in relation to Britishness since my collection of essays, *Not Easy Being British: Colour, Culture and Citizenship* came out in 1992. From my point of view the most important is that the suggestion, as made in that book, that the issue of racial equality led inevitably to the bigger questions and 'isms' of multiculturalism, national identity and re-thinking secularism is now commonplace. Very few made these connexions in the late 1980s and early 1990s when those essays were written. Most racial egalitarians thought that 'multiculturalism' was not sufficiently challenging of racism, that it did not cut very deep into society as it was merely about 'steelbands, saris and samosas'. The idea that multiculturalism threatened social unity, let alone was subversive of western civilisation, however common it is now, was undreamt of at that time. Moreover, those who thought of themselves as political multiculturalists and did not think multiculturalism was primarily about black music, exotic dress and spicy food all saw British nationalism as the property not of the British people but of right-wing ideologues. Their main reaction to any talk of Britishness was to denounce it as reactionary and racist and/or to argue that as no one could define what they meant by 'British' in terms of necessary and sufficient conditions, the concept should not be used as it referred to a fiction, to something that did not exist. In this the multiculturalists and the antiracists were united, as indeed they were that secularism was intrinsic to anti-racism and multiculturalism.

It was these views that I was challenging twenty years ago. At the time I was in a very small minority, especially amongst racial egalitarians. The

1

essays of that book were written in my private time whilst I was working as an Equal Opportunities Officer at the London Borough of Hillingdon and then at the head office of the Commission for Racial Equality. I was forever being told that the issues I was raising were unnecessary, confused and divisive – above all that they had nothing to do with racial equality. The rest of my career has more or less been spent in proving this charge mistaken. I may not have got as many people to agree with all my substantive views as I would have liked but few now think that Britain can hope to be a society in which ethnic minorities are not stigmatised and treated unfavourably without a large scale discussion of multiculturalism, national identity and secularism.

In the late 1980s it was still not uncontroversial (especially amongst racial egalitarians) to say that most ethnic minority people actually wanted to be British, indeed that many wanted to be British more than some white people did, and that this particularly applied to Asian Muslims. It is good to see over the years that this too has been vindicated and the proposition is no longer as controversial as it used to be, though in the case of some Muslims some misunderstandings persist.

Another change since those days of course is devolution of power from Westminster to Edinburgh and Cardiff (and agreement to transfer powers back to Belfast when certain conditions have been met), and the decline in the frequency and intensity of identification with British identity relative to Scottish, Welsh, English and Irish. That is a very large topic but one I do not discuss here in any detail (though see chapter 9 on the celebrating of St. George's Day). For the developments I am most interested in relate to not territorial and national differences within Britishness but to post-immigration ethno-religious ones. Here the story is about the rise and fall, or at least mixed fortunes of a communitarian multiculturalism. The essays collected in this sequel to *Not Easy* record or unpack elements in this story.

Muslims and Multiculturalism

British Muslim identity politics was stimulated by the *Satanic Verses Affair*. It was a crisis that led many to think of themselves for the first time as Muslims in a public way. With any identity, for some it will be a background, while others will often foreground it, although much will depend on context. So it is with Muslims. Even with those for whom a

Muslim identity is in many contexts not just a background, it does not follow that it is the religious dimension that is most prominent': it can be a sense of family and community; or for collective political advancement, or righting the wrongs done to Muslims. We cannot assume that being 'Muslim' means the same thing to all. For some, being Muslim is a matter of community membership and heritage; for others it is a few simple precepts about self, compassion, justice and the afterlife; for others it is a worldwide movement armed with a counter-ideology to modernity; and so on. Some Muslims are devout but apolitical; some are political but do not see their politics as being 'Islamic' (indeed, may even be anti-'Islamic').

It is ironic that Muslims are experiencing the pressures to step up and be British in the same context in which members of other minorities might be coming to feel an easing of identity pressures and greater freedom to mix and match identities on an individual basis. Some of the most interesting developments are the emergence of organisations – the scale of which is currently still relatively small – which want to belong to the family of public Muslims but are thoroughly critical of a religious politics. What is particularly distinctive about them is the relative thinness of their appeal to Islam to justify their social democratic politics. They could just as easily seek to privatise their Muslimness but feel a socio-political obligation to do the opposite. There is a felt need to join the public constellation of Muslim identities rather than walk away from them. Some contemporary Muslim identity politics, then, responds pragmatically, treating being 'British Muslim' as a hyphenated identity in which both parts are to be valued as important to oneself and one's principles and belief commitments. Of course to bring together two or several identity shaping, even identity defining, commitments will have an effect on each of the commitments. They will begin to interact, leading to some reinterpretation on the different sides, a process that often leads to scholarly engagement with the Islamic intellectual heritage.

One of the key areas of renewal and reinterpretation has been equality and related concepts. This can be seen in debates about gender equality in which Muslim cultural practices and taken for granted assumptions have been subjected to severe critique through fresh readings of the Qur'an, the sayings and practice of the Prophet Muhammad and Muslim history, tracing the emergence of conservative and restricted interpretations at moments when other interpretations could and should have been favoured (Mernissi, 1991; Ahmed, 1992; Wadud, 1999).

Plurality is emerging as an important Muslim idea. Despite certain ideas that one might associate with Saudi Arabia or the Taliban, most Muslims have no theological or conscientious problems with multi-faith citizenship – after all the Prophet Muhammad founded just such a polity. The first organised, settled Muslim community was in the city of Madina which was shared with Jews and others and was based on an inter-communally agreed constitution. The late Zaki Badawi, one of the most learned Muslim theologians to have lived in modern Britain, once described it as the first example of a multicultural constitution in history in that it guaranteed autonomy to the various communities of the city (Badawi, 2003).

Islam has a highly developed sense of social or ethical citizenship, in which, in line with contemporary western communitarian thinking, duties as well as rights are emphasised. This is illustrated in one of the 'five pillars of Islam', namely, *zakat*, the obligation to give a proportion of one's income or wealth to the poor and needy. It has an inherent civic character for it is not simply a responsibility to one's kith and kin or to those known in face to face relationships, such as people in one's neighbourhood or at one's workplace; it extends to strangers, to an 'imagined community'. The idea that it needs a state to enforce social citizenship or religious law more generally is very much a post-colonialist theology that seeks to place the political over the legal (the *Sharia*). More recently, and chiefly from within Europe and North America, a strand of Islamic modernity counters this authoritarian tendency by positioning the *Sharia* not as a body of unchanging law, but as a set of ethical principles with legal conclusions that apply to specific places and times only and so have to be continually reinterpreted, thus placing the ethical over the legal and the political (Sardar, 1987 and Ramadan, 2005). It is an example of how scholarship can draw on extra-European heritages and reinterpret them in a context of a democratic citizenship.

As Muslims discuss these matters and as Muslim discourses become part of British debates, these matters will become more openly debated and political maturity could mean that when we seek Muslim voices or civic participants we will not seek exclusively one or even a few kinds of Muslims. This is easier to achieve at the level of discourses, more difficult in terms of institutional accommodation. But it is not impossible. Moreover, it is a positive virtue that there is internal variety within any group and that (organised) members of any one group will want to locate themselves in different parts of the representational landscape – secular, religious, close to government, distant from mainstream political parties – for that is true integration; new groups should have similar opportunities to old groups and will not need to conform to a special minority perspective.

So allowing Muslims to politically organise 'as Muslims' without any sense of illegitimacy and for them to raise distinctive concerns, to have group representation in political parties, trades unions, various public bodies and so on, means allowing Muslims to organise in ways they think appropriate at different times, in different contexts and for different ends. The result will be a democratic constellation of organisations, networks, alliances and discourses in which there will be agreement and disagreement, in which group identity will be manifested more by way of family resemblances than the idea that one group means one voice.

Where there is 'difference' there must also be commonality. That commonality is citizenship, a citizenship that is seen in a plural and dispersed way. Emphasising and cultivating what we have in common is not a denial of difference – it all depends upon what kind of commonality. Commonality cannot be taken for granted, both in the sense that it usually has to be worked at, but equally importantly it has to be the right kind of commonality. Hence difference and commonality are not either-or opposites but are complementary and have to be made – lived – together, giving to each its due. More than that, commonality must be difference-friendly and if it is not, it must be remade to be so. This does not mean weak or indifferent national identities; on the contrary multiculturalism requires a framework of vibrant, dynamic, national narratives and the ceremonies and rituals which give expression to a national identity. We can see that minority identities are capable of generating a sense of attachment and belonging, even a sense of a 'cause' for many people. If it is to be equally attractive to those people, therefore, multicultural citizenship needs a comparable counter-balancing set of emotions; it cannot be merely about a legal status or a passport.

A sense of belonging to one's country is necessary to make a success of a multicultural society. An inclusive national identity is respectful of and builds upon the identities that people value, and does not trample upon them. So integration is not simply or even primarily a minority problem. For central to it is a citizenship and the right to make a claim on the national identity in which negative difference is challenged and supplanted by positive difference.

We cannot afford to leave out these aspects of multicultural citizenship from an intellectual or political vision of social reform and justice in the twenty-first century. Rather, the turning of negative difference into positive difference should be one of the tests of social justice in this century.

Multiculturalism: past its sell-by date?
The essays assembled in this book make clear, I hope, why I believe that it is neither intellectually nor politically true that multiculturalism is out of date. The term 'multiculturalism' (no less than the terms 'integration' or 'assimilation') operate at or combine different levels. There is the sociological level which acknowledges the fact that racial and ethnic groups exist in society, both in terms of minorities being told they are 'different' but also from 'the inside'; that is to say, minorities having their own sense of identity. This is sometimes termed 'multicultural society' in order to distinguish it from political concepts. Then, secondly, there is the question of what should the political response be to that social reality. Assimilation is one response; liberal integration based on respect for individuals but no political recognition of groups is another; and multiculturalism is yet another response based not just on the equal dignity of individuals but also on the political accommodation of group identities as a means of challenging exclusionary racisms and practices and fostering respect and inclusion for demeaned groups. Moving beyond a focus on exclusion and minorities is a third level of multiculturalism, which is not just about positive minority identities but a positive vision of society as a whole – but remade so as to include the previously excluded or marginalised on the basis of equality and belonging. It is at this level that we may speak of

multicultural integration or multicultural citizenship (Modood, 2007; Parekh, 2000; Taylor, 1994).

This third level of multiculturalism, incorporating the sociological fact of diversity, groupness and exclusion but going beyond individual rights and political accommodation, is perhaps the level that has been least emphasised. Or at least that is how it seems to many whose understanding of multiculturalism, sometimes polemical but sometimes sincere, is that multiculturalism is about encouraging minority difference without a counterbalancing emphasis on cross-cutting commonalities and a vision of a greater good. This has led many commentators and politicians to talk of multiculturalism as divisive and productive of segregation.

This popular, as well as academic, critique of multiculturalism was evident in the 1990s, not just in countries that had never embraced multiculturalism, such as France and Germany, but also in those that had, such as the Netherlands and Britain. After the terrorist attacks in America on 11 September, 2001 and their aftermath, including the London bombings of 7 July 2005 and other failed or prevented attacks in Britain, fears about international terrorism and associated wars and conflict coalesced with anxiety about Muslims failing to integrate in Britain and other countries. The anti-multiculturalism discourses came to not just dominate the relevant policy field but to be at the forefront of politics. Discourses of 'community cohesion' and 'integration' were prominent in this politics, which overlooked the fact that no major theorist or advocate of multiculturalism, nor any relevant policy or legislation, had promoted 'separatism'. Theorists of multiculturalism such as Taylor, 1994 and Parekh, 2000, related policy documents such as the CMEB, 2000 and enactments such as those in Canada, universally regarded as a pioneer and exemplar of state multiculturalism, all appealed to and built on an idea of national citizenship. Certainly some urge a 'post-national' analysis of society and advocated transnationalism or cosmopolitanism (eg Soysal, 1994; D A Jacobson, 1997; Held, 1995), but they are not multiculturalists in the sense being discussed here. Hence, from a multiculturalist point of view, though not from that of its critics, the recent emphasis on cohesion and citizenship, what has been called 'the civic turn' (Mouritsen, 2006), is a necessary rebalancing of the political multiculturalism of the 1990s, which largely took the form of what I called the second level of multiculturalism (Meer and Modood, 2009)[2]. It cannot be understood as simply a move from multiculturalism to integration, as it not only continues to understand exclusion and identity as sociological facts but also to continue with group consultations, representation and accommodation.

The latter have actually increased. The British government has found it necessary to increase the scale and level of consultations with Muslims in Britain since 9/11, though it has been dissatisfied with existing organisations and has sought to increase the number of organised interlocutors and the channels of communication. Avowedly anti-multiculturalist countries and governments have worked to increase corporatism in practice, for example with the creation by Nicholas Sarkozy of the French Council of the Muslim Faith (*Conseil Francais du Culte Musulman*) in 2003 to represent all Muslims to the French government in matters of worship and ritual; and by the creation of the *Islam Confrenz* in Germany in 2006, an exploratory body, yet with an extensive political agenda. It cannot be denied that these bodies are partly top-down efforts to control Muslims or to channel them into certain formations and away from others; but nevertheless its quite clear that such institutional processes cannot be understood within the conceptual framework of assimilation or individualist integration. In contrast, British Muslims have not been offered nor sought a single formal institutional basis such as the Islam Conference of the German government or the Council of Muslims of the French. The British arrangements are instead a mixture of semi-formal and ad hoc and are a part of an extended minority-majority relations that I have referred to as 'multiculturalism' (though the term has become unfashionable in Britain, as elsewhere in Europe).

The multiculturalism that I refer to has no single legal or policy statement (unlike Canada) but has grown up, sometimes in contradictory ways, in response to crises as well as mature reflection, and so is evolutionary and multi-faceted. The 'multi' is an essential feature of what I am talking about, for the policy and institutional arrangements have grown out of and continue to be part of ways to address not just Muslims but a plurality of minorities. The 'multi' does not merely refer to the fact that a number of minority groups are within the frame but also to the fact that different **kinds** of groups are being referred to. Some groups are defined by 'race' or 'colour' (eg black or Asian), some by national origins (eg Indian or Pakistani), some by religion (eg Sikh or Muslim) and so on. Indeed, the origins of British multiculturalism, both as an idea and as policies, lie in the experiences of African-American struggles for equality and dignity. British racial equality thinking and policy was directly and consciously influenced by developments in the USA in the 1960s and early 1970s. The policy paradigm was referred to as 'race relations' and the group on which policymakers were most focused was young black men. As the South Asian origin population became more numerous, more visible and more assertive, especially in relation to their cultural community needs, the terms 'ethnicity', 'ethnic minorities' and 'multiculturalism' replaced 'race' in an effort to better capture the changing reality. It is important to remember, however, that the foundations of Muslim-nonMuslim relations in Britain are based upon white-nonwhite relations and that no British policymaker (or social scientist) understood 'coloured immigrants' from the Commonwealth in terms of religion or expected, let alone desired, religion to have political significance.

The new political relevance of religion has not come from the state or 'top-down' but from the political mobilisation of specific minorities or parts of minorities who prioritised their religious identity over that of ethnicity and 'colour' (which is not to say that they deemed the latter insignificant). The Sikhs were the first religious minority to mobilise politically and win concessions from the state in relation to the legal recognition of the turban. So, in many ways, and as chapters 3 and 4 catalogue, Muslim political assertiveness arose in the context of an anti-racism movement, equality legislation and Sikh mobilisation – in short a political multiculturalism. Muslims, as late arrivals, have tried to catch up with the rights and concessions already won by racial and ethnic minority groups. It sometimes looks as if multiculturalism is a movement that Muslims have virtually taken over, though at the price of damaging the support for it – perhaps even mortally.

The event in which Muslim political agency first significantly manifested itself in Britain is over the battle of *The Satanic Verses* in the late 1980s (as elaborated in the next chapter). If we can get beyond 'the death sentence' and issues about freedom of expression, the Rushdie Affair revealed certain important characteristics about the politics of the emergent Muslim communities. Firstly, in line with what I have already said, Muslim politics was not created nor desired by the state but was a challenge to the existing majority-minority relations framework from below. Secondly, unlike most (but not all, *cf* the Sikhs) minority struggles up to that time, it consisted of the nominal and actual mobilisation of a single minority; Muslims neither looked to nor received support from other British minorities. They looked to the British establishment (publishers, the political class, the politicians, the law courts) to intervene on their behalf and some of them looked for allies amongst Muslim forces outside Britain. Thirdly, not only did the Rushdie Affair shift the focus of minority-majority relations from the Atlantic to 'the Orient' but it marked the beginning of the internationalisation of British minority-majority relations on a scale never achieved through pan-black or 'global South' solidarities. Global 'subaltern' politics had arrived in Britain, but in ways that few advocates of global activism had envisaged or desired. As much as it has provided a resource in a potential trans-national or 'ummatic' solidarity, this international association has also made life difficult for British Muslims (from Khomeini's *fatwa* to terrorist networks).

Fourthly, the Rushdie Affair threw up both a radical and a pragmatic 'moderate' leadership amongst Muslims in Britain. Evidence of the latter is how the UK Action Committee on Islamic Affairs (UKACIA), the main Muslim umbrella body thrown up by the campaign, initially depicted the offence which had angered Muslims as apostasy. Soon realising that this achieved little comprehension amongst the political class, let alone sympathy, however, they used the more British term, 'blasphemy', and when that too failed to rally support, they spoke of 'incitement to religious hatred', directly paralleling existing legislation in Northern Ireland (and incitement to racial hatred in Britain).

Yet, fifthly, the pragmatists were never able to decisively defeat the extremists, who continued to have some on-going presence. There was and is no centralised authority in British Islam (or for that matter in Islam *per se*, especially Sunni Islam) such that access to that authority was sufficient to lead Muslims. Muslim leaders who spend their time criticising extremists not only find themselves giving undue publicity to the extremists (whose salience is dependent on the fact that they are such popular hate figures in the media, which cannot leave them alone) but are criticised by the main body of Muslims for being divisive and not focusing attention on getting concessions from the state. It has also to be said that there is something about British Muslim political culture, reminiscent of left-wing student politics of the 1970s, which has a 'holier-than-thou' quality, in which it is easier to win approval for radical political rhetoric rather than practical compromises.

I mention these five features of the Muslim campaign against *The Satanic Verses* because they are all present today. Nevertheless, the pragmatic Muslim politics has been relatively successful in achieving the goals it set itself. The lead national moderate organisation, UKACIA, which later broadened out into the Muslim Council of Britain (MCB, founded in 1998) came to be accepted as a, if not *the*, voice of Muslims by the government and other bodies. It became the chosen interlocutor and, as domestic and international crises affecting British Muslims became more frequent and rose up the political agenda, it came to have more regular access to senior, up to the very top, policy makers across Whitehall than any other organisation representing a minority, religious, ethnic or racial, singly or collectively. The MCB's pre-eminence began to suffer from the mid-2000s, as it grew increasingly critical of the invasion of Iraq and of the so-called war on terror. The government started accusing it of failing to clearly and decisively reject extremism and sought alternative Muslim interlocutors.

From the early 1990s to that point, UKACIA/MCB lobbied primarily on four issues. The first was mobilising and getting a Muslim religious community voice, not subsumed under an Asian or black one, heard in the corridors of national and local power, and that UKACIA/MCB should be the voice of that community. Second was getting legislation on religious discrimination and incitement to religious hatred. Third was getting socio-economic policies targeted on the severe disadvantage of Bangladeshis, Pakistanis and other Muslim groups.

Finally, the fourth was getting the state to recognise and resource some Islamic schools. All four of these goals have been partly met. With none are we where we were in 1997 when New Labour came into power, though, as noted, there continues to be a problem about representativeness and this relates particularly to issues of foreign policy and security.

Nevertheless, despite these latter concerns that have come to throw many of the basic issues within the equality agenda into the shade, the Muslim equality agenda has got as far as it has because of the liberal and pragmatic political culture of this country on matters of religion, as opposed to a more thoroughgoing secularism that requires the state to control religion (see chapter 11). Moreover, Muslims utilised and extended previously existing arguments and policies in relation to racial and multicultural equality. By emphasising discrimination in educational and economic opportunities, political representation and the media, and 'Muslim-blindness' in the provision of health, care, and social services; and arguing for remedies which mirror existing legislation and policies in relation to sexual and racial equality, most *politically active* Muslims in respect of domestic issues have adjusted to and become part of British political culture and British multiculturalist politics in particular (chapter 7 explores in detail what some key Muslim community advocates think of multiculturalism in this country).

These, then – the accommodation of Muslims into a distinctively British multiculturalism – with all the tensions and conflicts this process has entailed and may continue to entail, are the subjects of the essays collected in this book. They were mostly written for non-academic audiences and were often engagements with public controversies during 2006 -2010. The next chapter, however, goes back to the time of *Not Easy Being British* but was not included in that earlier collection. As one of the first articles on the Rushdie Affair to be published in any journal, it sets out my original understanding of that conflict and its implications for 'race', equality and Britain, and has since guided my thinking on these topics.

Notes

1 Perhaps to even talk about a 'religious' dimension is already to be thinking of Islam in terms of a western, Protestant originating category (Asad, 2003), though one that many Muslims, western and others, have by now made their own.

2 Even in the 1990s, multiculturalism in Britain was sometimes expressly linked to a national identity, to its modernisation, to, for example, 'Cool Britannia' and 'rebranding Britain' (Leonard, 1997). Perhaps it is fair to say that the most serious multiculturalist public document produced, CMEB 2000, tried, somewhat inconsistently to simultaneously link multiculturalism to rethinking 'the national story' and to the 'post-national'.

1

British Asian Muslims and the Rushdie Affair

From *The Political Quarterly*, April 1990[1]

In 1989 'Rushdie' became a racial taunt in Britain. Prison warders were reported as reading passages from *The Satanic Verses* (hereafter *SV*) to a Muslim prisoner, and racial tension and racist attacks in Muslim/Asian areas increased. While some Muslims saw 'the Rushdie affair' in terms of the Crusades,[2] liberal intellectuals, while deploring the growing racism, saw it as a call to arms on behalf of the Enlightenment. Whatever the cause – racism, liberalism or passionate biblio-philia – no minority in the context of British race relations has been as friendless as Muslims in spring 1989 (not helped of course by their failure to disassociate themselves from the Ayatollah's *fatwa*) (Modood, 1989). Yet Muslims did not crumble in the face of this widespread and at times hysterical opposition. They unashamedly remained indignant, regardless of the reputation of infamy that their anger gave rise to (Akhtar, 1989). Where, one has to ask, did that anger and defiance come from?

Muslims in a European Society

There are now probably over a million Muslims (ie people born and brought up as Muslims) in Britain and this figure is bound to grow if for no other reason than that Muslims are much younger than the rest of the population and have large families. About two-thirds are of South Asian origin: over 400,000 from Pakistan, perhaps 120,000 from Bangladesh and up to 100,000 each from India and East Africa. The remainder are from the Middle East (120,000 Arabs, 75,000 Turks and Cypriots, 50,000 Iranians) and a small number from black Africa. While it would be foolish to suppose that all these form a single religiopolitical group it ought not to be overlooked that they form part of a larger European presence. The number of Muslims in both France (primarily N. African Arabs) and West Germany (mainly Turks) is more than double that in the UK and the total in the European Community is over six million.[3] The anti-*SV* street demonstrations were largely confined to the UK and achieved their intensity by the passion of a South Asian Islam missing in other countries, but it would be false to suppose that the conditions for Muslim action are singular to Britain. The depth of French Arabophobia, where cultural-racism has a greater intensity than colour-racism, and the current celebration of German ethnicity suggest the very opposite – indeed, the row in France about the right of Muslim girls to wear headscarves in state schools has been dubbed 'the French Rushdie affair'. Our own Rushdie affair should therefore not be seen as a pathology or as a once-and-for-all matter but as the first of what will probably be a series of major political battles to determine the shape of the rights of Muslims in European society – and, indeed, as part of the international struggle between a hegemonic West and rebellious Muslims reviving from a slumber with dreams of past glories.

I shall confine my attention to UK South Asian Muslims, and particularly the Pakistanis settled in fairly large-sized communities in towns and cities such as Bradford and Birmingham. It may be an exaggeration – though not a wholly wild one – to suppose that they represent the leading edge of a six-million force in Europe but it is undeniable that it is they who are the force behind the *SV* demonstrations both nationally and internationally, that they are the most charged with Islamic fervour and that they are the group that British society is currently being forced to adjust to or defeat.

Throughout the 1980s, of the nine non-white groups identified in the Labour Force Survey, Pakistanis and Bangladeshis have suffered the highest rates of unemployment, have the lowest number of educational qualifications and the highest profile in manual work; and this is true in each respect not just for women but also men, and not just for the middle-aged (the first generation) but also the young. They have had the most adverse impact from immigration laws and rules, they have the worst housing and suffer from the highest levels of attacks on person and property. Of all groups Pakistanis are least found in London and the South-East for they came mainly to work in the run-down mills and factories of the North and Midlands and have in consequence suffered most from the 'shake-out' of the early 80s and benefitted least from the recent growth. If a racial underclass exists in Britain, here it is.

The first step in understanding the anti-*SV* militancy is to recognise that we are talking about a semi-industrialised, newly urbanised working class community that is only one generation away from rural peasantry. For despite the explanations offered by the pundits – political manipulation, fundamentalism or even unqualified racism – it is an incontrovertible fact that the demonstrations and the book-burnings were above all spontaneous working-class anger and hurt pride. How can it be that the most socially deprived and racially harassed group should bear all this and explode in anger on an issue of religious honour? Socio-economic categories, like sociologically reductive conceptions of race and racism, barely begin to help us understand the phenomenon (For an example of sociological reductivism see Malik, 1989). To do that it is necessary to make at least a brief incursion into ethnic history, for the explanation lies in a deep-rooted conservatism and a religious devotionalism that cannot be picked up by an ahistorical sociology or a purely materialistic history.

Besieged Conservatism

The Muslim world has created many historical empires and its relation to the West has not always been that of an inferior; on the contrary, continental Europeans can remember a time when they trembled before the conquering might of Islam, and Muslims can remember when Europe was synonymous with backwardness and they were the leaders in civilisation and technology, one of the legacies of which was the renaissance of Western Europe. It has, like any civilisation, faced major epochal challenges. In the early medieval period it was a theological intellectualism. It was defeated by the establishment of a dogmatic unifying Islam which proved disastrous for philosophical, critical and, ultimately, religious thinking, the price of which is paid to this day. In the early modern period the problem came to be conceived by many as

15

one of eclecticism. It was felt by many, such as Shah Waliullah of Delhi (1703-64), that the spread of Muslim power and the mass conversions had brought into Islam a wide range of beliefs, superstitions, religious practices and social customs of the new Muslims and of conquered peoples such as the Hindus, such that Islam was no longer the simple, rational, anti-idolatrous, egalitarian faith that had made history. In this sense of impurity and decline are the origins of the major modern reform movements: fundamentalism and modernism. Each insisted on the need to break with historically received orthodoxy and to return to a fresh study of the Qur'an and the Prophet as exemplar either in order to re-enact it and shut out all other influences (fundamentalism) or in order to distil its universal message from its historical manifestation so as to apply it to new historical circumstances (modernism).

It is worth noting, if only to puncture the arrogance of European progressivism, that Islamic enlightenment in the form of Shah Waliullah's historical contextualism preceded its European counterpart. These reform movements were, however, born at a time of political weakness: Muslim power in India was being threatened by the rising religious and political militancy of the Hindu Marathas and the Sikhs (itself partly a reaction to Islamic re-assertiveness) and within the next 100 years virtually the whole Muslim world was to come under European hegemony and, in the case of India, colonial rule.

From that point onwards Muslim thought, whether reformist or conservative, was mixed up with a response to the West. Modernist reform came to mean acceptance of existing political realities and adoption of a Western framework of ideas. The response of the more orthodox as well as the uneducated, on the other hand, was a retreat into a dogmatic citadel in order to hold on to something uncorrupted by the West in the context of comprehensive political subordination. For the first time in history the Muslim world found itself in the realm of ideas totally unable to defend itself against the aggressor, let alone to impress the aggressor with any form of living, as opposed to historical, brilliance. In the last two centuries Islam, in so far as it was capable of putting up any show at all, seems to have lost all the intellectual and ideological battles. Yet it has survived. Its survival and resilience lay in the fact that its masses were not easily overawed by the new civilisation. It survived in the stubborn conservatism of the religious establishment and the ordinary people, above all the peasantry, who retained, indeed nourished, a collective memory of Islamic hegemony. They hung on to their Islam by a blind adherence to custom, tradition and religion.

The price of this defiant conservatism which allowed little space for critical thought has been little, slow and hesitant renewal of internal traditions, and only a superficial encounter with Western ideas, for the latter have not been seen as a resource but a threat. Forms of behaviour of course outlive their usefulness (nationalism in Western Europe is a good example) but it does not mean that they automatically disappear (Ulster is a good example). People nurtured over generations in a be-sieged conservatism cannot easily give it up (my father can remember when preachers in Delhi denounced electricity as un-Islamic; he therefore is disturbed but not surprised when he hears sermons against television – the medium, not the message – in Brent). They are unlikely to give it up where they perceive Western secular hegemony to be un-defeated and certainly not when it is audaciously contemptuous and stridently intolerant of their core values. They will not be tempted into lusher pastures when they experience, on the one hand, racist rejection and violence, and on the other hand pressures to change fast and into a culture that they deem to be decadent and a mortal enemy to Islam and decency.

Continuity and Change

Before we look further into the religious – political make-up of the British Asian Muslim, especially Pakistani, community it would be use-ful to bear in mind some other indicators of whether distinctively Asian attitudes are or are not being reproduced in Britain. For the kind of defensive traditionalism I am postulating is obviously not confined to religion in any narrow sense; if Asian Muslim attitudes are undergoing change on a wide front then religion will not be immune, and, con-versely, if those attitudes are showing relatively small shifts between generations this too will have implications for the whole of community relations. I do not have the space to review it here but there is now con-siderable and growing evidence that on a whole range of issues to do with sex, gender roles, arranged marriage, mixed marriages, female dress, family authority and honour, extended family and preservation of cultural identity second generation attitudes are closer to those of their parents' and hence to their peers in the sub-continent than to their British peers (see, for example, Anwar, 1986; Rex and Josephides, 1987; Shaw, 1988; *Daily Express*, 1989). Sex is absolutely central. In a secular, hedonistic society sex is usually seen as a paradigm of pleasure and of self-chosen relationships, some of which may turn out to be serious. Asian and especially Asian Muslim views are typically pre-modern. While Asian culture has a strong strain of romantic fantasy (most notably evidenced in films) the primary use of sex is to sustain one's, and ultimately the groom's, family. One's happiness is typically not postulated as independent of one's family's wellbeing. The average Pakistani in Britain, for instance, feels a strong sense of not only belonging to an extended family but also to a *birādari* (kinship group) of which a branch is in Britain but the centre of which is in Pakistan (Shaw, 1988). Even where this feeling is relatively weak amongst the young that may be because they are young rather than because they are simply out-growing it: as they get married and slowly become involved in the financial affairs and decision-making of the *birādari* they may come to have a more palpable sense of belonging.

I do not want to exaggerate the continuity (for there is genuine change and adaptation) nor to encourage a static conception of culture (that would be false and a disservice to good community relations) nor to deny that there are a significant number of exceptions (middle-class London is full of them). The evidence, however, not only supports my general thesis but intimates a further interesting development. It is perhaps a cliche, post-Rushdie, to say that the 1960s liberal assump-tions about immigration and 'melting-pot' seem facile compared to the perceptiveness of Enoch Powell on, say, native English chauvinism and Asian community formation[4] (these can of course be separated from his prescription of massive repatriation or prophecy of racial war). What to date has been less noticed is how inappropriate the American three-generation model of immigrants (derived from white experience in a country that was not as a whole hostile to their presence) is to Asian experience in Britain. That model postulates that the immigrants slave and self-sacrifice to see their children succeed in the new country; the second generation assimilate and conform to succeed; the grandchil-dren, assured of acceptance and advancement, have a romantic yearn-ing for their ancestral roots. British racism, however, extorts such a high price for the success of the second stage that Asian teenagers – in Bradford, Brick Lane and Southall – are beginning to say 'so far it is we who have had to make all the changes, now it is the turn of the British to change to accept the fact of our existence' (see, for example, Alibhai, 1989:46-49). This new ethnic assertiveness is likely to be more than a teenage fashion for it arises from genuine social conditions and a sense of threat to identity and will challenge the stereotype that Asians are passive and accepting.

Deobandis, Barelvis and Fundamentalists

One cannot discuss British Muslim political perspectives without discussing 'fundamentalism'. It is the word on every lip and journalistic pen and it is what editors want to know about when they commission articles. I have three comments to make on fundamentalism. Firstly, I shall offer a definition; secondly, I shall contend that fundamentalism is virtually nonexistent amongst Asian Muslims and played an insignificant part in the demonstrations and book-burnings; and, finally, that there is a real likelihood that fundamentalism will now become attractive to a portion of Muslim youth.

The term 'fundamentalism' originally arose to describe the literalist attitude of certain American Protestant sects to the Bible. As such, it cannot be directly transposed on to Muslims for the vast majority of Muslims, including those in Britain, are Sunnis who, incidentally, owe no allegiance whatsoever to Shiite Ayatollahs, and who, unlike the Shia, take all passages in the Qur'an literally rather than metaphorically. I understand fundamentalism in Sunni Islam to consist of the following beliefs:

(i)   to recapture the essence of one's faith one needs to return to the source, namely the Qur'an and Prophet Muhammad as the perfect model of a Muslim in personal life and public affairs and to reject all other historical accretions and contemporary norms as un-Islamic;

(ii) this source is not just a moral vision or a body of ethical principles but a comprehensive and indivisible way of life and the sole legitimate basis for positive law in all its details, all social institutions and all aspects of personal life and with appropriate leadership and effort can be implemented in any time or place for it is of universal authority, eternally valid and yet capable of a single correct interpretation;

(iii) no modern society, including most if not all the Muslim states, is or is endeavouring to be Islamic and Muslims in all societies, especially where they are a majority, are under an obligation to work to create an Islamic state.

A Sunni fundamentalist, then, believes that Islam is a totally systematic, self-sufficient set of ideas that owes nothing to history and can be enacted in a single uniform way of life which is the life that God meant for humankind and which it is the duty of all Muslims to approximate to as much as possible and in as many spheres of life as the distribution of political power between Muslims and non-Muslims allows (though Muslims have a further duty to improve this distribution in favour of 'true' Muslims as circumstances allow).

My Sunni (in the British context, let's say Muslim) fundamentalist is undoubtedly an ideal type and the definition is offered as such and not as a set of necessary and sufficient conditions.[5] Nevertheless, I believe that my definition is far superior to the popular usage when the term usually means no more than 'militant Muslim' or perhaps simply: 'Watch out, Muslims about!' The idea that a militant Muslim is a fundamentalist is on the same level of political analysis as that Neil Kinnock's Shadow Cabinet is Marxist! I doubt if there are more than a few thousand fundamentalists in Britain and most of them are likely to be in London rather than Bradford, in offices rather than factories. Asian fundamentalists are urban, educated and middle-class; British Asian Muslims have rural peasant origins and are only now coming to a point where they can produce individuals for whom the ideological rigour of fundamentalism and studied rejection of Western ideas is attractive and possible. If then the angry book-burners are not fundamentalists, what are they?

The majority of Pakistanis in this country are Barelvis; the majority of the remainder are Deobandis. Both these sects have their origins in the reformist movement set in motion by Shah Waliullah but came into existence in post-1857 British India. They were concerned with ways of maintaining Islam as a living social force in a non-Muslim polity and ruling culture. The Deobandis, taking their name from a school founded in Deoband, near Delhi, came to focus primarily on education and on keeping alive in the seminaries Muslim medieval theological and juristic doctrines. They saw politics as an unequal struggle and tried to be as independent as possible of the British state. Their anti-Britishness took the form of withdrawal and non-cooperation rather than of active confrontation but they took great care to shut out not only British and Hindu influences but also Shia. Through active proselytisation they built up a mass following as well as an international reputation in Islamic learning and more recently a worldwide organisation called Tabligh-i-Jamaat. It is represented in Britain with a national headquarters in Dewsbury, West Yorkshire, and has an active presence in Birmingham. The Deobandis currently show all signs of remaining true to their traditions that a good Muslim should seek in-depth knowledge of the doctrines of Islam, create a self-sufficient community and strengthen the faith of or convert lost souls. The Deobandis have no notion of an Islamic state and studiously avoid a clash with the powers that be.

The Barelvis are more numerous nationally, form the core of Bradford's Muslim working class and are part of the traditions of Sufi mysticism and Indian folk-religions. Deriving their name from Ahmed Riza Khan of Bareilly (1856-1921) theirs is an Islam of personalities; the Prophet Muhammad, for instance, is imbued with a metaphysical significance and devotional reverence that goes well beyond what some would regard as orthodox and has been called 'the mythification of Muhammad' (Rahman, 1982:41). Their religious heroes are not confined to the Prophet and the early Arab Muslims but include a galaxy of minor and major saints who, contrary to more reformist Islam, can intercede with God on behalf of petitioners. Additionally they hold dear many customs and superstitions that have no justification in the Qur'an but have been acquired from other sources, usually from the rich soil of India, and are no doubt a reminder of the religion of their forefathers before conversion to Islam during the period of Muslim rule. Their easygoing Islam (in matters of doctrine and worship; they are even more puritanical on matters of sex than other Muslim sects) is also reflected in attitudes to politics.

While, unlike the Deobandis, they are not apolitical they, unlike the fundamentalists, have no political grand plan; under the Raj they co-operated with and were favoured by British rule, were not at the fore-front in the Independence movement and it has been said that 'flexibi-lity is a feature of their behaviour' (Robinson, 1988:10)[6]. Their religious passion is usually aroused when their doctrines and forms of worship are denounced by Deobandis and fundamentalists as un-Islamic his-torical accretions. This intense sectarianism has led to and continues to lead to serious violence in Pakistan and there are not many towns in England which have mosques and have not witnessed such a clash.

The leading fundamentalist movement in South Asia, the Jamaat-i-Islami, was founded in 1941by Sayyid Abul Ala Mawdudi (1903-1979), one of the leading and most influential Muslim thinkers of this century. My earlier definition of fundamentalism sums up this philosophical outlook. In Pakistan Jamaat is both a religious movement and an overt political party with a highly authoritarian Leninist cadre structure. While it has never made any electoral headway it has come to be a force in the universities and the education system, in the officer ranks of the army and civil service. Mawdudi's ethical vision and intellectually syste-matic representation of Islam were attractive to the idealistic educated young when in contrast the Westernised ruling and commercial class, while paying lip-service to Islam, not only seemed to offer no alterna-tive ethical vision of society, but seemed to lack standards of public service and personal morality. It has been said of the first decade of Pakistan's history that 'the liberals are strong [ie are in power], but liberalism is weak' (Smith, 1957:236). The remarks fit not just the country as a whole but the liberals themselves: not only did they fail to impress their outlook upon the country but their personal convictions were too weak even to guide their own behaviour.

With this background of religious backwardness at the bottom and secular hypocrisy and selfishness at the top Mawdudi, with a Platonic contempt for democracy, tried to create an authentic Islamic intel-ligentsia to rival the existing Westernised one. Jamaat became the lead-ing ideological force amongst the non-Westernised urban middle and lower-middle classes of Pakistan with influence and support in many other Muslim countries, above all in the Egyptian Muslim Brotherhood and the Saudi Arabian establishment from whom it has received generous funding. Originally composed of idealists with high standards of personal integrity, its agitprop tactics played a key role in thrusting Islamic issues into the centre of Pakistani politics, but came to involve it increasingly in social disorder and the toppling of governments. As a result, on the one hand the leadership of the Jamaat in the 1970s and 80s passed into non-ideological hands and it became extremely thuggish with university branches becoming gun-toting fascist paramilitary organisations (Alavi, 1987:94-95). On the other hand, under Zia, the leadership became part of the circle of government and Jamaat enjoyed considerable government patronage and moved from religious radicalism to become an archconservative religious legitimiser of a military dictatorship (Binder, 1986:262). The Jamaat is represented in Britain by the Islamic Foundation in Leicester and the UK Islamic Mission. It is very small in number compared to the Deobandis or Barelvis and has negligible working class community links, but with Saudi money and support it is better nationally and internationally organised than the other two. Its two organisations are avowedly propagandistic and represent as far as I can tell the old-style idealism, but within the constraints of Saudi political and international interests.

Pragmatism and Religious Politics

South Asian Muslims, especially Pakistanis, in Britain are then represented by three tendencies: Deobandi apolitical conservative revivalists, Barelvi devotionalists with a pro-British Raj history and a small network of Saudi-backed middle class fundamentalists. How is it then that they can be portrayed as a radical assault upon British values, a threat to the state and an enemy to good race relations? Informed opinion seems to be that Muslims put the dogmas of Islam above a value for the norms of political conduct and debate as developed in a civil society; that Muslims insist on mixing up religion and politics. There is however far more error than truth in this as once again a quick glance at Pakistan will show.

The Pakistani electorate is as thoroughly pragmatic and non-ideological as it is possible to be. Pakistanis think it unthinkable that politics should challenge what after all is the grounding of their society, Islam; but they do not expect politics to be deduced from religious propositions or read out of texts. They see Islam as the core of their cultural heritage and a source of national identity rather than as a rule-book to be put into practice. They expect a harmony at some abstract level between Islam and politics (as we all expect a harmony between ethics and politics) but have no ideological formula for how to bring this about and they certainly have never desired the state to be led by religionists. Hence the consistently poor showing of the Jamaat and other religious parties in every election and the absence of popular support for Zia's Islamicisation[7]. The ambivalent and pragmatic understanding of the relationship between religion and politics that I am pointing to is well illustrated by the fact that though Z. A. Bhutto found it necessary to call his political programme *Islamic Socialism,* he in fact won the 1970 election on a socialist platform despite 113 fatwas against socialism (so much for the power of fatwas in politics; and these, unlike in the Rushdie case, were decrees of their own spiritual leaders, not a Shiite Ayatollah). The Barelvis, I might add, no less than the Deobandis, steadfastly take the view that spiritual mentors (*pirs*) have no right to pronounce on political matters (Alavi, 1987:85-86).

This pragmatic approach is very evident in the participation of Asian Muslims in British politics as has been acutely observed by John Rex (1988). Rex recognises the different sectarian strands amongst Muslims in Birmingham (its 80,000 Muslims are the single largest settlement in Britain), but argues that while all are deeply antipathetic to British sexual habits and modes of family life and anxious about such influences upon their children from British schools; believe that Islam is a higher form of morality than that practised by most of the natives; are indifferent to ideological socialism and capitalism; they nevertheless are all deeply accommodationist when it comes to politics. The pragmatic approach in politics could not be better evidenced than by the fact that despite having a social ethic that is close to that of the moral right they overwhelmingly support the Labour Party as the best vehicle to defend their material interests. Rex concludes with the prediction that though the issue of schooling could become a difficult political issue, in general 'Muslim society in Britain will be characterised by a political quietism qualified by a drive to sustain and promote a distinctive type of marriage and family life'(Rex, 1988:217).

Based on the evidence of the mid-1980s, a time in any case when Asian Muslims were overshadowed by black activism and the emergence of

Indian economic success, this was a somewhat complacent but not an unreasonable conclusion. Judging by the conventional understanding of the Rushdie affair one would suppose that the fault in Rex's analysis was that he failed to make allowance for fundamentalism. In fact the anger against *SV* had nothing to do with fundamentalism – or indeed Khomeni. Virtually every practising Muslim was offended by passages from the book and shocked that it was written by a Muslim of whom till then the Asian community were proud. Rushdie has argued that the *mullahs* whipped up the ordinary Muslims for their own political motives (Rushdie, 1989). The truth is that all the religious zealots had to do was simply quote from *SV* for anger, shame and hurt to be felt. It is important to be clear that *SV* was not objected to as an intellectual critique of their faith (libraries are full of those); for the average Muslim the vulgar language, the explicit sexual imagery, the attribution of lustful motives – without any evidence – to the holy Prophet, in short the reduction of their religion to a selfish sexual appetite[8], was no more a contribution to literary discourse than pissing upon the Bible is a theological argument.

While it was a member of staff of the Islamic Foundation in Leicester that first alerted the Muslim world to the book (and while in Britain quiet representations to the publishers and the government were made by the middle-class Asian and Arab Muslims of London), it was not until the Bradford Barelvis picked up the issue that the public registered something was up. The passion and intensity of the street demonstrations was a product of Barelvi devotionalism, which normally even other Muslims think is excessive in the exalted status it confers on Muhammad. It was the cultists not the Calvinists that were the driving force of the protest – and more by their example than by any national organisation. While just about the whole of Britain was denouncing the fundamentalists, in fact the Sunni fundamentalists, either of their own will or because of Saudi pique at Iran, were amongst the first to begin to tone things down (see, for example, *Impact International*, 1989:10-12). As for the Shia fundamentalists, their fewness in number and lack of organic links with the wider Muslim community here makes them incapable of taking the lead.

What perhaps cannot be denied and is worth noting is that by his intervention the Ayatollah rose in Asian estimation. Not because the majority wished Rushdie killed, let alone wanted to kill him. It was because he was considered to have stood up for Islamic dignity and sensibilities against the West and in contrast to Arab silence. Initially, Asian Muslims had looked to Saudi Arabia as the spiritual leader of Sunni Islam to speak out. They were baffled by the silence and dismayed when they recalled the trouble that that government had gone to to prevent the showing of *Death of a Princess* on British television: were the Guardians of the Holy places more concerned with the honour of the royal family than of Muhammad?[9]

The group Asian Muslims felt most let down by, however, was the London secular Asian intelligentsia (a minority only of whom are Muslim, of course). Not only did they not even attempt to act as an intermediary and prevent a polarisation – the least that they could have done – but some of their leading lights joined the public vilification of Muslims. Collective declarations were issued deploring the actions of 'fundamentalists' and groups were set up with titles such as 'Women Against Fundamentalism' thus reinforcing the dismissive tactic that all assertive or angry Muslims were just extreme fundamentalists. By using the media's language they reinforced a racist stereotype of Muslims as fundamentalists, which, if excusable in those who have no firsthand knowledge of Muslims, in Asians and Muslims was shocking. It reveals the frightening power of media caricatures over knowledge gained by direct acquaintance. Of course the shock of the *fatwa* led to confusion and mistakes on all sides, and an understandable fear for the life of Salman Rushdie emotionally clouded many a judgement. Nevertheless the ease with which the popular stereotypes of Muslims found a home in the minds of the Asian intelligentsia reveals a profound division which may well have long-term consequences which Britain may come to regret. In any case the creation of an Anglicised middle/intellectual class which does not understand or feel responsible for its own ethnic working-class is, I believe, the single most worrying trend in the Muslim and other Asian communities.

I argued earlier that the opportunity for fundamentalism in Pakistan arose from the inadequacies of an intelligentsia that had cut itself off from its roots and that the initial fundamentalist project was to create an alternative intelligentsia that was rooted in Islam rather than in Western culture. My expectation is that this too, in so far as it is possible in a Western society, will be the focus of Muslim fundamentalist activity here. Reports from all over the country suggest that Asian Muslim youth are deserting the bars and clubs and returning to the mosques and religious classes. By the summer of 1989 it was the youths who were marching in the streets and looking for action though their initial reaction had been cooler than their fathers'. With the education and social experience that Britain has given them and will give those who are currently at school they may well find the faith of their parents too simple in its devotionalism and too accommodating in its political outlook. As Francis Robinson (1988:20) has incisively argued, we should

> expect support for the Jamaat in Britain to be proportionately rather greater than in Pakistan. First because here all Muslims are confronted directly by the challenges of Western civilisation, and to these the Jamaat offers the most complete and systematic answer. And second because Muslims in Britain are favourably placed sociologically. Religious fundamentalism seems to flourish amongst those who are in a state of transition from one society to another.

The Rushdie affair was the hour of the simple devotionalist; we may yet have the hour of the educated fundamentalist. Nature abhors a vacuum and the desertion of the secular intelligentsia has created one. No longer can they be looked to as role-models let alone for moral leadership; their example, instead, is being used by the traditionalists as further evidence of how 'Westoxification' corrupts. My personal view, however, is that fundamentalism, at least as a political force, say, as an Islamic party, will remain as an ideological fringe and will continue to suffer from its dependency upon the ultra-conservative, indeed, feudal Saudi Arabian establishment. One of the many unfortunate consequences of *SV* may however be that the not unreasonable assumption that a couple of generations of experience in the West would lead Muslims, in line with the Jews, to develop a liberal modernist interpretation of their faith can no longer, to put it at its mildest, be taken for granted. Our philosophies of race relations will, however, I believe, be radically recast in the 1990s and Islamic reassertion and communalism will be one of the primary reasons. It is important that Muslims be in this debate. I would therefore like to devote my final section to considering critically some aspects of the concept of racial equality and minority status and their relationship to the Muslim experience.

Racial Equality and Minority Rights

'Fight racism, not Rushdie': stickers bearing this slogan were worn by many who wanted to be on the same side as the Muslims.[10] It was well meant but betrayed a poverty of understanding. It is a strange idea that when somebody is shot in the leg, one says 'Never mind, the pain in the elbow is surely worse'. The root problem is that contemporary antiracism defines people in terms of their colour; Muslims – suffering all the problems that antiracists identify – hardly ever think of themselves in terms of their colour. And so, in terms of their own being, Muslims feel most acutely those problems that the antiracists are blind to; and respond weakly to those challenges that the antiracists want to meet with most force. And there is no way out of this impasse if we remain wedded to a concept of racism that sees only colour-discrimination as a cause and material deprivation as a result. We need concepts of race and racism that can critique socio-cultural environments which devalue people because of their physical differences but also because of their membership of a cultural minority and, critically, where the two overlap and create a double disadvantage (Modood, 1990).[11] Such concepts should help us to understand that any oppressed group feels its oppression most according to those dimensions of its being which *it* (not the oppressor) values the most; moreover, it will resist its oppression from those dimensions of its being from which it derives its greatest collective psychological strength.

For this and further reasons I shall come to below, Muslims cannot easily, confidently or systematically assume the moral high ground on the issue of colour-racism; their sense of being and their surest convictions about their devaluation by others comes from their historical community of faith and their critique of 'the West'. Authentic 'antiracism' for Muslims, therefore, will inevitably have a religious dimension and take a form in which it is integrated to the rest of Muslim concerns. Antiracism begins (ie ought to begin) by accepting oppressed groups on their own terms (knowing full well that these will change and evolve), not by imposing a spurious identity and asking them to fight in the name of that (Modood, 1988). The new strength amongst Muslim youth in, for example, not tolerating racial harassment owes no less to Islamic reassertion than to metropolitan antiracism: people don't turn and run when something they care about is under attack. The racist taunt 'Rushdie!' rouses more self-defence than 'black bastard!'

Muslims need to be part of the rethinking I speak of and at the same time must admit that they have something not only to teach but to learn from the antiracist, for Muslim thinking too is inadequate to the current situation (eg Hobohm, 1978). The Qur'anic teaching is that people are to be valued in terms of virtue not colour or race. Muslims insist that there is no divinely favoured race and that the Qur'an is God's message to the whole of mankind. They take pride in the fact that Islam is a genuine multiethnic religion (Christianity is the only other) and point to the fact that one of the first converts to Islam was Bilal, a black slave (Arab trade in black slaves having predated the same by Euro-peans) and that in Muslim history there have been several black rulers and generals in racially mixed societies. This then is the standard Mus-lim view on racial equality. Like all 'colour-blind' approaches it has two weaknesses.

Firstly, it is too weak to prevent racial and ethnic prejudice. While it was strong enough, unlike its Christian and secular Western counterparts, to prevent the development of official and popular ideologies of racism, it is not the case that Islam has banished racism. Arab racism is such that most Pakistanis would prefer to work in Britain than in Saudi Arabia for a higher income; racist humiliations from shopkeepers, taxi-drivers, catering staff and so on have become a regular feature of the pilgrimage to Mecca for the diverse ethnic groups of Islam. Asians have no fewer racial stereotypes about whites and blacks than these groups have about Asians or about each other.

The second weakness flows from the first. A 'colour-blind' approach is unable to sanction any programme of positive action to tackle the problem once it is acknowledged to exist. The 1976 Race Relations Act has provisions for, say, employers to identify under-representation of racial minorities in the workforce and to target within certain limits those groups for recruitment. It is not obvious that strictly Muslim thinking can consistently support this. Some very recent Muslim posi-tion statements seem to express a reluctance for, what is essential to positive action, heightening racial categories. Indeed, one goes as far as to say that 'we believe that it is very unhelpful to look at human rela-tions in Britain on the basis of race' (UK Action Committee on Islamic Affairs, 1989:11), while another asserts 'there is only one race, the human race' (Akhtar, 1989:9). This is, as I have said, because Muslims (and indeed most other minority communities) do not see themselves in terms of colour and do not want a public identity that emphasises colour. The way out is a concept of race that not only allows minorities a purchase upon their mode of being but, equally importantly, also upon how white British society defines them – that is to say upon their mode of oppression. While radical antiracists are as it were religion-blind and culture-blind, it would be foolish for a nonwhite group to not recognise the existence of colour-racism and how it, as well as culture-racism, affects them and their life-chances. For that would rob them of effective strategies as well as alliances with other nonwhite groups to oppose the various dimensions of racism and its effects. To develop such thinking one cannot – pace fundamentalism – rely solely on Qur'anic concepts.

I believe that we are slowly learning that our concepts of racial equality need to be tuned to not just guaranteeing that individuals of different hues are treated alike but also to the fact that Britain now encompasses communities with different norms, cultures and religions. Hence racial equality cannot always mean that our public institutions and the law itself must treat everybody as if they were the same – for that will usually mean treating everybody by the norms and convenience of the majority. Local authorities have been discovering this, especially with regards to schools, usually in the glare of adverse publicity, and English common law has quietly and sensibly gone a long way down this road (Poulter, 1986). Yet here, too, our thinking is far from clear. Some Muslims believe that the have the answer. What is urged is some variation of the *millat* system (as in the editorial of the *Crescent*, 1 June 1989): a form of religious-based communal pluralism which reached its most developed form in the Ottoman Empire whereby ethnic minorities ran their own communal affairs with a minimum of state interference. The British in India allowed the development of a Muslim family law with its own separate courts and much the same proposal was put to John Patten, the Home Office Minister with responsibility for community relations, by a Muslim delegation in the summer of 1989. The idea, hardly surprisingly, was rejected out of hand and I do not wish to argue for it. Nevertheless, I do think Britain can usefully consider aspects of Muslim historical experience for I do not think equality is possible without some degree of pluralism.

Once again dialogue, learning from a variety of traditions, is the way forward, for Muslim views of pluralism are as they stand not adequate either. They fail to confer equality of citizenship in some crucial respects. Islam insists on a fundamental equality between all Muslims; it insists on the rights of non-Muslims in a Muslim state to lead their lives according to their own norms and customs; it insists on the right of minorities to enjoy the full protection of the state; it does not however, even as an ideal, allow them to be senior members of the major branches of the state nor propagate an ideology which challenges that of the state, ie Islam[12]. Under Jamaat's influence Zia's Islamicisation went even further and created separate electorates so non-Muslims could not influence the election of Muslim legislators. Historically, Muslim minorities have accordingly sought a tolerance-cum-pluralism not formal equality; the UK offers its Muslims a formal equality but is not yet willing to acknowledge in its institutional and legal arrangements the existence of a Muslim community which for instance can be deeply hurt and provoked to violence by forms of literature that the majority of citizens have become used to tolerating. The question of the interrelationship between equality and pluralism lies, I believe, at the heart of future British race relations and it is one on which Muslim thought will and ought to focus.

For however appalled we might be by 'the hang 'em and flog 'em' interpreters of the Quranic verses that should not obscure for any of us, Muslims and non-Muslims, the long-term significance of the 'Rushdie affair'. What was at issue was not primarily the life of Salman Rushdie, for most Muslims rightly did not mean him physical harm, yet they did not believe that the argument ended there. Nor was it about freedom of expression *per se* for, on the one hand, most Muslims do not seek to limit freedom of inquiry and, on the other hand, just about nobody wants absolute freedom of expression including incitement to racial hatred. It is surely not Muslims alone who oppose the libertarianism which sees the artist as a Nietzschean *ubermensch*, towering above conventional morality with perfect liberty to publish imaginative explorations regardless of social consequences. For, indeed, the artist without social responsibility who provokes anger instead of dialogue threatens the field of discourse itself. The ultimate issue, however, that *The Satanic Verses* controversy posed are the rights of non-European religious and cultural minorities in the context of a secular hegemony. It is a time for self-discovery. Is the Enlightenment big enough to tolerate the existence of pre-Enlightenment religious enthusiasm or can it only exist by suffocating all who fail to be overawed by its intellectual brilliance and vision of Man?

Notes

1 From: *The Political Quarterly*, vol.61, no.2, April 1990, pp.143-160; with kind permission of John Wiley and Sons.

2 And more recently not only Muslims, see Johnson (1989). A Gallup Poll survey at the end of 1989 found that 37 per cent of those questioned thought an international conflict between Christians and Muslims likely in the new decade, *Sunday Telegraph*. 31 December 1989.

3 Anwar (1984). These are estimates for 1990. Twenty years later it is estimated that there are about 2 million Muslims in the UK, about 3 million in France, 4 million in Germany.

4 One particular phrase of Powell is lodged in my brain. It goes something like: 'When an Englishman looks into the face of Asia he sees whom he will have to contest for his land'. What is remarkable is that it was said at an early moment in the process of Asian immigration when commentators of all political complexions assumed that social conflict would take a white-black form.

5 My archetype is Abul Ala Mawdudi. See, for example, Mawdudi (1976; 1986).

6 This is the single most helpful guide on Asian Muslim groups in Britain. I am grateful to Francis Robinson, Phillip Lewis, Shabhir Aktar and John Rex for sharing their understanding of Muslim groups with me.

7 What little support the religious parties do receive is from the urban and town-based middle class not from rural Punjab and Mirpur where 95 per cent of Pakistanis in Britain are from (Esposito cited in Binder, 1986:341).

8 This is well brought out in Parekh (1989) – the first article in the British media that showed any understanding of the Muslim anger.

9 Hence placards such as 'Shame on Arab Leaders' and 'Ayatollah, You Will Never Walk Alone' have been evident at demonstrations.

10 Consider: 'Had Rushdie been white, the left would almost certainly have condemned [*SV*] as patronising prejudice against an already oppressed racial minority (Akhtar, 1989:110). It is because most Muslims believe this that they now consider (if they did not previously do so) the left's interest in racial minorities is only as a political pawn. I remember reading that there was the same feeling in Brixton when after the riots the left began arriving.

11 See Murphy (1987) for an excellent account of how racism is far more potent when it focuses on not just colour but also culture.

12 See, for example, the account of the minimum principles of an ideal Islamic state agreed to by a 1949 conference of all major sects in Pakistan (Brohi, 1979).

2

Muslim Integration and Secularism

From *Islam & Europe: Challenges and Opportunities*, 2006[1]

There is an anti-Muslim wind blowing across the European continent. One factor is the perception that Muslims are making politically exceptional, culturally unreasonable or theologically alien demands upon European states. Against that, I wish to say that the claims Muslims are making, in fact, parallel comparable arguments about gender or ethnic equality. Seeing the issue in that context shows how European and contemporary is the logic of mainstream Muslim identity politics. Additionally I shall argue that multicultural politics must embrace what I call a moderate secularism, and resist a radical secularism.

My main experience of these issues, both the lived experience but also in terms of research and intellectual reflection, is based upon Britain. But I believe this experience has relevance beyond Britain. Of course so many of these issues are becoming European issues, for at policy level there is convergence as well as divergence, and moreover our countries impact upon one another. We saw that so dramatically at the start of 2006, with the Danish cartoon affair, which became a multinational affair, having an impact domestically in a number of countries, including those some distance from Denmark.

In Britain we have to come to approach issues to do with Muslim integration through what we used to call – and in other countries the language will not always have a natural resonance or fit – 'race-relations', which is an American term. We are of course talking about the post-war migration of non-Europeans into a European country, or from the global South to the global North. And this phenomenon in Britain, initially at least, was very much understood with American ideas. People saw the issue as primarily one of colour racism, which of course had a historical legacy: slavery, colonialism, empire, and so on. The whole issue to do with Muslims, which is a headline issue today, only became a feature of majority-minority relations from the early 1990s. In Britain nobody talked about the Muslims in the 1980s. The big dramatic crisis that brought the idea of Muslims into public political discourse was the 'Satanic Verses' or Salman Rushdie affair in 1989-90.

Up to that time, and to some extent beyond that time, the dominant post-immigration issue was colour racism. One consequence of that is that the legal and policy framework in Britain still reflects the conceptualisation and priorities of racial dualism, of black-white dualism. Muslims and issues about Muslims arose in that context, and have struggled to seek clarity and a distinctive set of priorities by counterposing themselves in that context, against that agenda. This dependence upon a 'race' framework has meant, at least initially, that Muslims have been marginalised. To some extent the assertiveness of Muslims in Britain has to be understood in the context of trying to move themselves from a marginalised position where things were seen in terms of black and white, to one where they say 'talk to us as Muslims, treat us as Muslims, not just as people who are not white'.

Moreover, in this Atlantocentric version of racism, which is certainly one of the classical and enduring versions, phenotype explains the existence of certain cultural traits (Miles, 1989:71-72). These traits are mainly negative in the case of blacks, people of African descent. As a result, racism or racial discrimination comes to be thought of as unfavourable treatment on the grounds of 'colour'. I refer to this as 'colour-racism'. While the physicality of blacks is taken to be enough to fill out the image of them as a group, as a 'race' – as for example, strong, sensual, rhythmical and unintelligent – the racialised image of Asians is not so extensively linked to physical appearance. It very soon appeals to cultural motifs such as language, religion, family structures, exotic dress, cuisine and art forms (Modood, 1997). These are taken to be part of the meaning of 'Asian' and of why Asians – which in Britain means

South Asians – are alien, backward and undesirable. Such motifs are appealed to in excluding, harassing or discriminating against Asians – in both constituting them as a group and justifying negative treatment of them. Muslims too are, indeed, being generalised about in these and other ways in Europe (and elsewhere) at the moment. They are being perceived not just as neighbours, citizens and so on but as Muslims; and it has to be said that many Muslims – like some blacks, Jews, gays, women, Scots etc in parallel situations before them – are vociferously challenging the negative perceptions but not the underlying logic that Muslims are a group. They are responding to the negative perceptions by offering positive images, stories and generalisations about Muslims; less often by saying Muslims are not a group but a variety of individuals, citizens etc. Hence a process of group-formation is well underway.

Why do I call this process 'racialisation' and the negative dimension of it 'anti-Muslim racism'? Because the 'otherness' or groupness' that is being appealed to and is being developed is connected to the cultural and racial otherness that is connected to European/white people's historical and contemporary perception and treatment of people that they perceive to be non-European or non-white. How Muslims are perceived today is both connected to how they have been perceived and treated by European empires and their racial hierarchies, as well as by Christian Islamophobia and the Crusades in earlier centuries (Daniel, 1961 and 1967). The images, generalisations and fears have both a continuity as well as a newness. Moreover, these perceptions and treatments overlap with contemporary European/white people's attitudes and behaviour towards blacks, Asians, immigrants and so on. The perception and treatment clearly has a religious and cultural dimension but equally clearly it has a phenotypical dimension. Given a number of images – cartoons – of people and asked to pick out a Muslim, most people would have a go and not reply but I do not know what any of these people believe, just as if they were asked to identify Jews they would have a go (though probably less today than in the past – because Jews are becoming de-racialised, normalised as 'white', in some parts of the west).

It is true that 'Muslim' is not a (putative) biological category in the way that 'black' or 'South Asian' or Chinese is. But nor was 'Jew' once: a long, non-linear history of racialisation turned a faith-cum-ethnic group into a 'race'. More precisely, the latter did not so much as replace the former but superimposed itself. No one denied that Jews were a religious community with a distinctive language(s), culture(s) and religion but they also came to be seen as a race – and with horrific consequences. Similarly, Bosnian Muslims were 'ethnically cleansed' by people who were phenotypically, linguistically and culturally the same as themselves because they came to be identified as an 'ethnic' or a 'racial' group. The ethnic cleanser, unlike an Inquistor, wasted no time in finding out what people believed, if and how often they went to a mosque and so on: their victims were 'ethnically' identified as Muslims. My argument is that this same kind of process – though at least so far at a much lower level of violence – is taking place in western Europe and, I would hazard, in the United States, given public support for 'racial profiling' at airports and by security services etc.

The results of such racialisation or ethnicisation is not 'pure' racism, ie it is not just biological or phenotypical, which it might be said to be in the case of people of African descent. But it is clear here that Muslims are not exceptional, as the above example of the Jews illustrates. As I have already suggested, the same is true of the most numerous non-whites in the UK, namely people of south Asian origin, locally called 'Asians' (and less pleasant monikers). I have argued (Modood, 2007) that even before the rise of a distinct anti-Muslim racism there was an anti-Asian racism and that it was distinct from anti-black racism in having distinct stereotypes (if one was unintelligent, aggressive, happy-go-lucky and lazy, the other was 'too clever by half', passive, worked too hard and did not know how to have fun). Moreover, if in the case of black people the stereotypes appealed to some (implicit) biology, to IQ, physical prowess, sense of rhythm, sexual drive and so on, none of the main stereotypes about Asians even implicitly referred to a scientific or folk biology. The stereotypes all referred to Asian cultural norms and community structures – to gender roles and norms, patriarchy, family authority and obligations, arranged marriages, religion, work ethic and so on. So anti-Asian racism is best understood as *cultural racism*. The most violent form of racism that Asians in Britain have experienced is random physical attacks in public places, 'Paki-bashing'. I have not seen any analysis of this phenomenon that refers to any biological beliefs held by the perpetrators. Interviews with the pool of people from which the perpetrators come – young working-class white males, especially 'skinheads' – and others in their neighbourhoods accuse Asians not of a deficient biology but of being aliens, of not belonging to 'our country', of 'taking over the country' and so on (Bonnett, 1993:19-20; Cohen 1988: 83; Back, 1993). Actually, of things that the Nazis accused Jews of – as well as of not having the right biology (Meer and Noorani, 2008).

Once we break with the idea that (contemporary) racism is only about biology or that racism is of one classical kind, then the idea of a pure racism should lose its social science appeal. We should be able to see that cultural groups and religious groups can be racialised; that Muslims can be the victims of racism *qua* Muslims as well as *qua* Asians or Arabs or Bosnians. Indeed that these different kinds of racisms can interact and have a dynamic and so can mutate and new forms of racism can emerge (Modood, 2005: 6-18 and chapter 1). This understanding enables us to see the historic co-existence of colour- and cultural-racisms, how it has affected different groups ('races') in different ways, with sometimes one and sometimes the other being dominant. It also enables us to trace and identify how a racism dominant at one time (such as colour-racism in the 1950s) can be overtaken by another, such as cultural-racism in the 1990s. Such changes can be the context for new conflicts and new identity assertiveness. These shifts are part of the background of why so many Muslims felt that a 'race relations' focus on colour-racism and colour-identities was capturing neither how they were devalued in contemporary Britain nor generating the solidarities that resist that devaluation (*cf* the British Muslim magazine, *Q-News*; Bari, 2005). The major issue in which this was first crystallised was the protest against Salman Rushdie's novel, *The Satanic Verses*, at the end of the 1980s, when larger numbers of Muslims were mobilised than had hitherto been in relation to racism, and which received very little support from other non-whites, as discussed in chapter 1.

Identity Politics

The second American influence I want to draw attention to is the idea of positive identity. The colour-blind humanism of Martin Luther King Jr, whose philosophy could be expressed as 'black, white, we're all the same under the skin', came to be mixed with an emphasis by some of his young successors on black pride and black autonomy. A similar development took place in Britain. We moved from thinking of issues to do with race or 'coloured' minorities as just something to do with skin-colour to people wanting to affirm certain marginalised or suppressed identities. Or people creating new identities, manufacturing identities as a way of negotiating a position of equality and dignity for themselves in the contemporary context.

I think it's best to see the development of what one might call racial explicitness and positive blackness – that is to say people saying 'I am black' as opposed to us pretending that equality means that we never notice whether people are black or white – as part of a wider socio-political climate which is not confined to race and culture, or non-white minorities. Feminism, gay pride, various kinds of minority nationalism in Europe are all examples of new identity movements which have become an important feature in many countries. Especially in those countries in which class politics has declined in salience. Some of these identities have a territorial face such as Flemish, Basque, Scottish or Quebecois, but there are other movements that don't talk about a territory: gender identity, gay pride, and ethnic minority identities for example. These identities have become particularly marked in Anglophone countries. In fact it would be fair to say that what is often claimed today in the name of racial equality, again especially in the English speaking world, goes beyond the claims that were made in the 1960s. Iris Young, the American feminist philosopher, expressed well the new political climate, when she described the emergence of an ideal of equality, based not just on allowing excluded groups to assimilate and live by the norms of dominant groups, but on the view that 'a positive self-definition of group difference is in fact more libratory' (1990:57).

So this is a difference-affirming notion of equality, rather than a kind of 'we're all the same under the colour of the skin' notion of equality. And this significant shift, from colour-blindness to difference assertion, takes us from an understanding of equality in terms of individualism and cultural assimilation to a politics of recognition, recognition of other identities, to equality as encompassing public ethnicity. This perception of equality means not having to hide or apologise for ones origins, family or community, and requires others to show respect for them. Public attitudes and arguments must adapt to encourage this heritage rather than expect it to wither away.

So we have here two concepts of equality which can be stated as follows: firstly the right to assimilate to the majority or dominant culture in the public sphere, with toleration of difference in the private sphere. The second concept of equality is the right to have one's difference, like minority ethnicity, recognised and supported in both the public and the private sphere. While the first represents a classical liberal response to difference, the latter is very much the take of the new identity politics. The two are not however alternative conceptions of equality in the sense that to hold one, the other must be rejected. Multiculturalism properly construed requires support for both conceptions, so it is not a question of having to choose between one or the other, but expanding the first to include the second. The assumption behind the first is that participation in the public or national culture is necessary for the effective exercise of citizenship. And that the only obstacle to this are the exclusionary processes preventing gradual assimilation. The second conception too assumes that groups excluded from the national culture have their citizenship diminished as a result, and sees the remedy not in rejecting the right to assimilate, but in adding the right to widen and adapt the national culture and the public and media symbols of national membership to include the relevant minority identities.

It can be seen then, that the public-private distinction is crucial to the contemporary discussion of equal citizenship and particularly to the challenge of an earlier liberal position. It is in this political and intellectual climate, namely a climate in which what would earlier have been called private matters have become sources of equality struggles, that Muslim assertiveness emerged as a domestic political phenomenon. In this respect the advances achieved by antiracism and feminism, with its slogan 'the personal is the political', acted as benchmarks for later political group entrants, such as Muslims. So, while Muslims raise distinctive concerns, the logic of their demands often mirrors those of other equality seeking groups. One of the current conceptions of equality, then, is difference-affirming equality, with related notions of respect, recognition and identity, and this is what I understand by political multiculturalism (Modood, 2007).

Religious Equality

Now what kinds of specific policy demands are being made by or on behalf of religious groups and Muslim identity politics in particular, when these multiculturalist ideas are deployed? I suggest that these political demands, which I put under the rubric 'religious equality' have three dimensions, which as it were, get progressively thicker. They start off minimally but in getting bigger they are progressively less acceptable to radical secularists. Very briefly, these three sets of demands are firstly, that there should not be religious discrimination. That is the easiest to understand and presumably very few people will want to disagree with it. For instance, an employer should not prefer a candidate, or disfavour a candidate on the basis of that person being of a particular religious background, or of no religious background (except where a religion is a genuine occupational qualification).

The next step up in the demand for religious equality is even-handedness between different religions in relation to native religion. By this I mean that newly settled religious groups, like Muslims, Hindus, Sikhs and so on, will say 'If Protestants or Catholics or Jews are allowed certain access to resources or certain institutional representation, then this should be extended to the new religions. 'Even-handedness' (Carens, 2000) captures this sense of equality because of course, there will always be some difference of scale; for instance Christians might form 75 per cent of the population, Muslims might form 4 per cent of the population. We can not have a numerical equality, but even-handedness means treating both sets of groups in the same way in terms of their recognition, in terms of their rights to enjoy public space, public resources such as the school system, the delivery of welfare services, provision in relation to hospitals and the army and so on.

Thirdly, religious equality might mean the idea of positive inclusion of religious groups. That would be quite a thick idea of equality, but – and this is my argument – it parallels the claims that are made in relation to gender equality, racial equality and so on. It is not a distinctively religious argument, let alone a distinctively Islamic argument. The basic idea is that we measure equality in society by a number of ways, but one way is by the degree to which all people, regardless of religious background, are equally represented as the recipients of the benefits and opportunities that society has to offer. In Britain, borrowing from the

United States for decades now, we have what we call 'ethnic monitoring'. That is to say, we record some kind of ethnic self-definition of, for example, candidates for jobs, and we compare that to their success rate in getting jobs, to see whether being, let's say African-Caribbean, has any impact on the likelihood of, say, their being employed in the national health service or the police, or a university and so on. So, if we do that for race and gender, and of course gender is monitored in this way across most of the countries of the European Union, then why should we not do that for religious groups?

Let me give a specific example: the BBC currently believes it is of political importance to review and improve its personnel practices and its output programmes, including its on-screen representation of the British population by making provision for, and winning the competence of, three particular categories of people. For a few years now various policies have been targeted at improving the position in relation to three particular population groups: women, ethnic groups and young people. Why should it not also use religious groups as a criterion of inclusivity, and help to demonstrate that it is doing the same for viewers and staff defined by religious community membership? That would really be taking religion as a measure of inclusivity, just as we take these other measures.

Implications for Liberal Citizenship

The multiculturalism or politics of difference that I am advocating has four major implications for liberal citizenship. Firstly, it is clearly a collective project, and concerns collectivities, and not just individuals. Secondly, it is not colour-, gender-, sexual orientation-blind, and so breeches the liberal public-private identity distinction, which prohibits the recognition of particular group identities. Thirdly, it takes race, sex and sexuality beyond being merely ascriptive sources of identity. For liberal citizenship, race is of interest only because no one can choose their race, and so should not be discriminated against on something over which they have no control. This is the classical liberal position. But if equality is about respecting previously demeaned identities, and most of our equality discourse is of that kind today, for example, in taking pride in ones blackness, rather than in accepting it merely as a private matter, then what is being addressed in anti-discrimination or promoted as a public identity, is a chosen response to one's ascription, it is not merely an ascriptive category. Exactly the same applies to sex and sexuality: we may not choose our sex or sexual orientation, but we choose how to live with it politically. Do we keep it private, or do we make it the basis of a social movement, and seek public resources and representation for it? Some gay people say 'yes', other people say 'no', so a public identity has a certain element of choice; it's not merely ascriptive.

That leads me to the fourth point, which is in fact felt by liberals to be the greatest challenge. Muslims and other religious groups are now utilising the kind of identity recognition arguments I have been discussing, and claiming that religious identity, just like gay identity and just like certain forms of racial identity, should not just be privatised and tolerated but should be part of the public space. In their case, however, they come into conflict with an additional fourth dimension of liberal citizenship that we can refer to by 'secularism'. By secularism I mean the view that religion is a feature, perhaps uniquely, of private, not public identity. It expresses itself in the response that women, black and gay are ascribed, unchosen identities, while being a Muslim is a chosen belief; once you start talking about a religious identity like Muslim, you're no longer talking about the politics of recognition, difference and equality, because all those things (gender, sexuality, race) are not chosen, whereas religion is something one can walk away from.

I think this extreme secularist response is sociologically naïve, and to some extent it's a political con, a political bad faith argument, because the position of Muslims in countries like ours today is similar to the other identities of difference, as Muslims catch up with and engage with the contemporary culture of equality. No one chooses to be or not to be born into a Muslim family. Similarly, no one chooses to be born into a society where to be a Muslim, or to look like a Muslim creates suspicion, hostility or failure to get the job you applied for. Though how Muslims respond to these circumstances will vary. Some will organise resistance while others will try to stop looking like Muslims, the equivalent of what in America has been called 'passing for white'. Some will build an ideology out of their subordination, others will not, just as a woman can choose to be a feminist or not. Again, some Muslims may define their Islam in terms of piety rather than in terms of politics, just as some women may see no politics in their gender, while for others their gender will be at the centre of their politics.

So my argument is that we should include Muslims in this arena of marginalised identities that are claiming equality and public space. There is not a category division between gender, race, ethnicity, sexuality on the one hand, and Muslims on the other. Those who see the current Muslim assertiveness as an unwanted and illegitimate child of multiculturalism have only two choices if they want to be consistent: they can repudiate the idea of equality as identity recognition, and return to the 1960's liberal idea of equality as colour-, sex-, religion-blindness. (Barry, 2001). If it is the latter that is adopted, then it should be consistent with gender-blindness, colour-blindness, sexual orientation-blindness, not merely single out religion. Or at least we need an explicit argument that equality as recognition does not apply to oppressed religious communities, perhaps uniquely not to religious communities. To deny Muslims positive equality without one of these two arguments is to be open to the charge of double standards. Hence, a programme of racial and multicultural equality is not I believe possible today without a discussion of the merits and limits of secularism. Secularism can no longer be treated as 'off limits', or as former president Jacques Chirac said in a major speech in 2004, 'non-negotiable'.

Secularisms

Not that it's really a matter of being for or against secularism – that's too simple – but rather a careful, institution by institution analysis, of how to draw the public-private boundary and further the cause of multicultural equality and inclusivity. For this public-private boundary is not as simple as it seems. What seems appropriate in one country can be regarded as very inappropriate in another country. While all western countries are clearly secular in many ways, their interpretations of secularisms and the institutional arrangements which give substance to it diverge according to the dominant national religious culture, and the different projects of nation-state building. So it may be a universal idea, but it takes a number of not just different but contradictory forms.

For example, the United States's first amendment to the constitution, that there shall be no established church has wide support in that country; and in the last two decades, there has been a tendency amongst academics and jurists to interpret the church-state separation in more and more radical ways (Sandel, 1994; Hamburger, 2002). Yet, as is well known, not only is the US a deeply religious society with much higher levels of church attendance than in western Europe, but there is a strong Protestant, even evangelical fundamentalism, that is rare in Europe. This fundamentalism disputes some of the new radical interpretations of the 'no establishment' clause, though not necessarily the clause itself. And it is one of the primary mobilising forces in American politics. It is widely claimed that it decided the presidential election of 2004. The churches in question – mainly white, mainly in the South and Midwest – campaign openly for candidates and parties. Indeed they raise large sums of money for politicians, and introduce religion-based issues into politics, such as positions on abortion, HIV-Aids, homosexuality, stem-cell research, prayer at school and so on. It is said that no openly avowed atheist has ever been a candidate for the White House, and that it would be impossible for such a candidate to be elected. It is not at all unusual for politicians, in fact for president George W. Bush it was most usual, to talk publicly about their faith, to appeal to religion, and to hold prayer meetings in government buildings.

On the other hand, in 'establishment' Britain bishops sit in the upper chamber of the legislature by right, and only the senior Archbishop can crown a new head of state, the monarch, yet politicians rarely talk about their religion. British politicians exercise reticence and guard their privacy about religion, which is seen to be part of the profession of politics. It was noticeable, for example, that when Prime Minister Blair went to a summit meeting with President Bush to discuss aspects of the Iraq War in 2003, the US media widely speculated that the two leaders had prayed together. Yet Prime Minister Blair, one of the most openly professed and active Christians ever to hold that office, refused to answer questions on this issue from the British media on his return, saying it was a private matter. Indeed, Blair's press officer, Alastair Cambell, famously declared on that occasion: 'We do not do God.' Questioned later about this, Blair said: 'I don't want to end up with an American-style type of politics with us all going out there and beating our chests about our faith' and observed that while people were defined by their faith, it was 'a bit unhealthy' if it became used in the political process

(BBC, 2005). So what in America is regarded perfectly fine for presidents to do, in Britain is regarded as 'unhealthy'. The British state may have an established church, but the beliefs of the Queen's First Minister are his own concern.

France draws the distinction between state and religion differently again. Like the US, there's no state church, but unlike the US, the state actively promotes the privatisation of religion. While in the US organised religion in civil society is powerful and seeks to exert influence on the political process, French civil society does not carry signs or expressions of religion. Yet the French state, contrary to the US, confers institutional legal status on the Catholic and Protestant churches, and on the Jewish consistory, albeit carefully designating organised religion as 'cultes' and not communities. So we have a situation where in England or Britain, we have a very weak establishment and religion is weak in civil society, but not absent – it can lead campaigns for nuclear disarmament, third world debt relief, peace movements and so on. In the US, establishment is constitutionally prohibited, but religion is strong and is politically mobilised. And then thirdly, in France, we have an actively secular state, which offers top-down recognition, and yet religion is weak in civil society – indeed, in many ways, it is kept out of civil society. The contrast between these forms of secularisms are summarised in Table 1. I include the divergent relationship of faith schools and the state to reinforce the point I have been making.

Table 1: Religion vis-à-vis State and Civil Society in three Countries

	State	Religion in Civil Society
Britain	Weak establishment; with state funding and incorporation of faith schools.	Weak but churches can be a source of political criticism and action
United States	No establishment; tax relief for private faith schools.	Strong and politically mobilised
France	Actively secular but offers top-down recognition and control; state payments to private faith schools.	Weak and it is rare for churches to be political

Adapted from Modood, 2007

So, given this kind of diversity, which is not confined to the three cases discussed here (the diversity gets more and more multiple the more cases we look at), what are the appropriate limits of the state? It seems that we can all be good secularists but we disagree on what are the appropriate limits of the state. Everyone will agree that there should be religious freedom, and that this should include freedom of belief and worship in private associations. That is more or less a universal position, excluding a few places like Saudi Arabia, which of course does not claim to be a secular polity. Family, too, falls on the private side of the line, but the state regulates the limits of what is a lawful family. For example, polygamy is not permitted in many countries, not to mention the deployment of official definitions of family in the distribution of welfare-entitlement. Religions typically put a premium on mutuality, on mutual aid, and on care of the sick, the homeless, the elderly and so on. They set up organisations to pursue these aims – but so do states. Should there be a competitive or cooperative relationships between these religions and state organisations, or do they have to ignore each other? Can public money raised out of taxes on religious as well as non-religious citizens not be used to support the organisations favoured by some religious taxpayers?

And what of schools? Do parents not have the right to expect that schools, while pursuing border educational civic aims, will make an effort not to create a conflict between the work of the school, and the upbringing of the children at home, but rather show respect for their religious background? Can parents, as associations of religious citizens, not set up their own schools, and should those schools not be supported out of the taxes of the same parents? Is the school where the private meets the public or is it, in some platonic manner, where the state takes over the children from the family and pursues only its own purposes?

Even if there is to be no established church, the state may still wish to work with organised religion as social partner, as in the case of Germany, or to have some forum in which it consults with organised religion, some kind of national council of religions, as in Belgium. Or even if it does not do that, because it is regarded as compromising the principle of secularism, political parties, being agents in civil society rather than organs of the state, may wish to do so, and institute special representation for religious groups, as many do for groups defined by age, gender, region, language, ethnicity, and so on. What is wrong, for example, with having a Muslim section in the Labour Party, or the Christian Democrat Party? Why is that a breach of principles but not so when we do this for other identity groups?

It is clear, then, that the idea of the public is a multifaceted concept and, in relation to secularism, may be defined differently in relation to different dimensions of religion and in different countries? We can all be secularists then, all approve of secularism in some respect, and yet have quite different views, influenced by historical legacies and varied pragmatic compromises of where to draw the line between the public and the private, because these lines are often contingent and pragmatic, not deduced from an abstract principle. It would be quite mistaken to suppose that all religious spokespersons or at least all political Muslims are on one side of the line, wherever that line is, and all others are on the other side.

There are many different ways of drawing the various lines of that issue. In the past, the drawing of them had reflected particular contexts, shaped by differential customs, urgency of needs, and sensitivity to the sensibilities of the relevant religious groups. Where the lines are in Belgium, or the Netherlands or in Britain, has not been arrived at by an abstract ethical principle, blind to society. They have been made to work by working with the sensibilities of the relevant populations. Exactly the same consideration of relevance and sensitivity is needed in relation to the accommodation of Muslims in Europe, not a battle of slogans and ideological oversimplification. So multicultural equality, when applied to religious groups, means that secularism *simpliciter* appears to be an obstacle to pluralistic integration and equality. But secularism pure and simple is not what exists in the world, so the obstacle is just an ideological or an imaginary obstacle. The country-by-country situation is, as we have seen, more complex and indeed far less inhospitable to the accommodation of Muslims than the ideology of secularism might suggest.

Religious Identities and Equality

Let me summarise the approach that I think we should take. Firstly, I am arguing for a reconceptualisation of equality from sameness to an incorporation of respect for difference. Secondly, I am arguing for a reconceptualisation of secularism from the concept of neutrality and a strict public-private divide to a moderate and evolutionary secularism, based on institutional adjustments which takes account of the sensibilities of religious people and so varies from country to country. Thirdly, let us take a pragmatic, case by case, negotiated approach to dealing with controversy and conflict as it arises, because this is what we have done historically, and not some kind of ideological view that says Muslim demands are unreasonable because they breach some fundamental principle of secularism. So this institutional integration approach is based on including Islam into the institutional framework of the state, using the historical accommodation between state and church as a basis for negotiation, in order to achieve consensual resolutions, consistent with equality and justice. Since these accommodations have varied from country to country, it means there is no exemplary solution, for contemporary solutions too will depend on the national context, and will not have a once and for all time basis, because we are actually always revising these matters. It is clearly a dialogical perspective and assumes the possibility of mutual education and learning.

For example, the recognition of Islam in Europe can take a corporatist form, can be led or even imposed by the state in a top-down way, and therefore can take a church or ecclesiastical model as its form, and I think it does sometimes. This may be appropriate for certain countries at certain moments, and could be, usually is, consistent with the conception of multiculturalism. However, it's not ideal, and it would not be my own preference. It would not represent the British multicultural experience and its potentiality at its best. Corporate inclusion would require Muslims and their representatives to speak with one voice, when that is not typical of at least Sunni Islam, and certainly is not typical for South-Asian Sunni Islam as practiced by a majority of Muslims in Britain. My own preference would be for an approach that is less corporatist, less statist and less churchy, in brief, less French. Because I think that is what is typical of the French model: that it is corporatist, statist and actually very churchy, even though the French think they have secularism at the heart of it.

An approach in which civil society played a greater role would be more comfortable with there being a variety of Muslim voices, representatives and groups. Different institutions, organisations and associations would seek to accommodate Muslims in ways that worked for them best at a particular time, knowing that these ways may, or ought to, be modified over time, and Muslim and other pressure groups and civic actors may be continually evolving their claims and agendas. Improvisation, flexibility, consultation, learning by – to use American expression – 'suck it and see' and by the example of others, incrementalism, and all the other virtues of a pragmatic politics in close touch with a dynamic civil society can as much and perhaps better, bring about multicultural equality, than a top-down corporatist inclusion.

So representation here would mean the inclusion of a diversity of backgrounds and sensibilities, not delegates or corporate structures. Recognition then, must be pragmatically and experimentally handled, and civil society must share the burden of representation. In my preferred approach it would be quite likely that different kinds of groups, Muslims, Hindus and Catholics for instance, let alone women, gays and different ethnic minority groups, might choose to organise in different ways, and to relate to key civic and political institutions in different ways. While each might look over its shoulder at what the others are doing or getting, and use any such precedent to formulate its own claims, we should on this approach not require symmetry, but be able to live with some degree of what we might call variable geometry. I am unable to specify what this degree of flexibility might be, but it should be clear that sensitivity to the specific religious, cultural and socio-economic needs in a specific time and place, in a political context, is critical to multiculturalism. This indeterminacy leaves something to be desired, but I hope it is evident that it can be a strength too. It also underlines that multiculturalism is not a comprehensive political theory, but can and must sit alongside other political values and be made to work with varied institutional, national and historical contexts.

The emergence of Muslim political agency has thrown British multiculturalism – and its European equivalents – into theoretical and practical disarray. It has led to policy reversals in the Netherlands and elsewhere, and across Europe has strengthened intolerant, exclusive nationalism. We should in fact be moving the other way, and enacting the kinds of legal and policy measures that are necessary to accommodate Muslims as equal citizens in European polities. These would include anti-discrimination measures in areas such as employment, positive action to achieve a full and just political representation of Muslims in various areas of public life, the inclusion of Muslim history as European history, and so on. Critically, I have been arguing that the inclusion of Islam as an organised religion, and of Muslim identity as a public identity are necessary to integrate Muslims and to pursue religious equality. While this inclusion runs against certain interpretations of secularism, it is not inconsistent with what secularism means in practice in Europe. We should let this evolving moderate secularism, and the spirit of compromise it represents be our guide (Modood, 2010). Unfortunately an ideological secularism is currently being asserted especially by centre-left intellectuals and generating European domestic versions of what one might call the clash of civilisation. That some people are today developing secularism as an ideology as a reaction to Muslim assertiveness is actually a challenge to both pluralism and equality, and thus to some of the bases of contemporary democracy. It has to be resisted no less than, say, the radical anti-secularism of some Islamists.

Note

1 From my chapter of the same name in *Islam & Europe: Challenges and Opportunities*, Leuven University Press, 2008: 85-112, with kind permission of the Leuven University Press.

3

ID-ology: Review of *Identity and Violence: The Illusion of Destiny* by Amartya Sen

From *Catalyst*, Jan/Feb, 2007:32-33

Amartya Sen is a Nobel Laureate in Economics so there is no doubting his intellectual prowess though on this occasion he has not only written outside his specialism but has written for the non-academic. Nor does this book draw much on the academic literature. This cannot be because he would have found it uncongenial. Sen's target are the contemporary political appeals to group identities, especially amongst some Muslims, which he thinks reduce the complexity and plurality of social relations and lived identities to a singularity. Yet this has been the dominant theme, indeed, the orthodoxy of the social theory and sociology of identities for over a decade. Critiques of homogenisation and lectures on multiple identities are a cliché in sociology. One difference between this literature and Sen though is that he emphasises, as economists are wont to do, individual choice, whilst sociologists focus on social factors; they highlight the variety of determining factors, such as class, gender, race, generation and so on. But ultimately this is perhaps a difference of degree than of kind, for in both cases the conclusion is the same: assertions of singular identities are sociological distortions and usually a product of prejudice (when ascribed to others) or of political projects (when directed at one's co-ethnics). Moreover, whilst at one time sociologists seemed to be running with the current of these political projects – feminism, black pride, gay liberation – now there is ambivalence.

Sen's own politics lie primarily in a high-minded cosmopolitanism and a concern for the global poor and needy but he has an Olympian view in which a sense of community and belonging are unwanted and unnecessary. In a typically American way he assumes that freedom is the highest ethical and political good, which tends to sideline equality (the term does not appear in the index). He is right, however, to see Islamism as more political than religious and to see it as a continuation of anti-imperialist global struggles against a hegemonic West, and that it can become crudely anti-Western. In this it is not atypical. Anti-imperialism, like other 'anti-' struggles can all too easily be framed by the ideologies they oppose. Sexism divides the world into men and women and antisexism can end up doing the same. Similarly, if some forms of racism see good-bad in the world in terms of white-black, so do some forms of antiracism with the good guys simply assuming a different colour.

While Sen is primarily concerned with Islamism he evokes for me some of my thoughts about political blackness, especially the Black Sections movement in the Labour Party in the 1980s and how I emphasised the importance of identities like Asian and Muslim to bring out the diversity of the minority experience. Some of these latter identities have of course come to be interpreted in dualistic ways, most notably Muslim/nonMuslim, and have eclipsed discussions of blackness. For Sen colour and racial identities are very much in the background ('black' is not in the index). One regrettable result is that racism – including anti-Muslim racism – features very little in Sen's understanding of identity and violence. This obscures one of the most important sources of reactive identity, of damaged identities, anger and violence. He has some insightful things to say about colonialism; eg about the importance of humiliation and not just economics and politics, but he does not fully see how for some people a religious (or racial) identity, the sense of a proud peoplehood that a historical religion can give to some people, can be central to this sense of humiliation and to fighting against it.

At times Sen appreciates the importance of 'recognition' of and respect for demeaned and devalued groups but this does not usually extend to Muslims, certainly not to the need for a 'Muslim Power' project to create a Muslim political agency or movement to reverse the ways in which Muslims are not in control of their own affairs even in Muslim-majority countries. I do, however, share his concern that, both in Britain and internationally, some Muslims are defining themselves too narrowly. Just like some other equality and self-determination struggles so some Muslims are boxing themselves in all kinds of ways by defining themselves in dualistic terms, as the West's 'other'.

Sen rightly deplores the kind of inward-looking multiculturalism which does not highlight the importance of interaction with people beyond one's group(s); such an attitude can lead to conformism, ignorance about and indifference to the concerns and sensitivities of one's fellow citizens and so to a diminished sense of the common good and even intolerance. Yet he does not see how in recent years some minorities have come to bear heavy blasts of prejudice and intolerance and told that they are unBritish. Take the recent so-called national debate about the face-veil. It is an object that is worn by about the same number of people as who wear reflective sun-glasses so that they can see you in ways you cannot see them, and so both can make other people uncomfortable in equal measure. But the face-veil debate has been used to abuse, harangue and bully Muslims in ways that make interactive multiculturalism difficult. Perhaps we need moral panics of this sort so that people can get things off their chest rather than bottle them up and project even greater resentment against the objects of their animus. But the price is a frightened and besieged minority community. An argument for interactive multiculturalism not just ignores this at its peril but at the cost of serious analysis.

The book is very wide-ranging and does not just have a current affairs focus; there are interesting historical discussions about the Muslim world, India, China and so on. In particular Sen brings out how each civilisation, including the West, has been dependent on the ideas, culture and technology of the others. In particular, that if in the last 500 years the flow has been from the West to the others, in the previous 1,000 years it was the other way round. Without the mathematics, science, technology and scholarship from China, India, Iran and the Arabs, the West would still be languishing in its Dark Ages. And who knows what the next 500 years will be like, as power once again shifts eastwards.

4

The Liberal Dilemma:
Integration or Vilification?

From *Open Democracy* website, 8 February, 2006[1]

The origins of the infamous Danish cartoons of the Prophet Muhammad do not lie in an attempt to offer contemporary comment, let alone satire, but the desire to illustrate a children's book. While such pictures would have been distasteful to many Muslims – hence why no illustrator could be found – the cartoons are in an entirely different league of offence. They are mostly unfriendly to Islam and Muslims and the most notorious implicate the Prophet with terrorism. If the message was meant to be non-Muslims have the right to draw Muhammad, it has come out as the Prophet of Islam was a terrorist.

Moreover, the cartoons are not just about one individual but about Muslims *per se*. Just as a cartoon portraying Moses as a crooked financier would not be about one man but a comment on Jews. And just as the latter would be racist so are the cartoons in question.

That does not in itself mean they should be banned. One relies on the sensitivity and responsibility of individuals and institutions to refrain from what is legal but unacceptable. Where these qualities are missing one relies on public debate and censure to provide standards and restraints. Hence where matters are not or cannot easily be regulated by law one relies on protest as well as empathy. This is how most racist speech and images and other free expressions (eg the use of golliwogs as commercial brands or *The Black and White Minstrel Show*) have been censured (rather than censored) away.

Sometimes legal intervention is also necessary. For example, when there is a serious risk of incitement to hatred; or when the 'fighting talk' is likely to inflame passions and risk public order; or when it is likely to reinforce prejudice and lead to acts of discrimination or victimisation. In recognition of this the British Parliament passed a bill on 31 January, 2006 to protect against incitement to religious hatred. Yet it was only passed after the Lords and the MPs – supported by much of the liberal intelligentsia – forced the government to accept amendments that weakened its initial proposals. The message was that incitement to religious hatred in Britain is a lesser problem than in Northern Ireland, so weaker legislation was sufficient. The kindest thing one could say about this analysis is that events in the world are testing it.

A key sticking point for the critics – that incitement must require the intention to stir up hatred – reveals a blind spot in liberal thinking that the Danish cartoon case amplifies. If the intention of the Danish news-paper *Jyllands-Posten* was not to cause offence, there clearly was a purpose of trying to achieve some kind of victory over Muslims, to bring Muslims into line – especially as it emerged that the same paper refused to print cartoons ridiculing Jesus because they risked giving offence to some Christians (Fouché, 2006).

The Danish editor cannot plead ignorance of what the effects on Mus-lims would be for the whole exercise was premised on the view that a collective effort involving twelve cartoonists was necessary to withstand Muslim opposition. As for the republication of the cartoons across parts of Europe, this was deliberately done to teach Muslims a lesson.

A Hole in the Mind

But the cartoons themselves are a trigger rather than the issue, for everyone – Muslims and non-Muslims – 'views' them (whether literally or imaginatively) in a wider domestic and international context that is already deeply contested. From the Muslim side, the underlying causes of their current anger are a deep sense that they are not respected, that they and their most cherished feelings are 'fair game'. Inferior protective legislation, socio-economic marginality, cultural disdain, draconian security surveillance, the occupation of Palestine, the international 'war on terror' all converge on this point. The cartoons cannot be compared to some of these situations but distil the experience of inferiority and of being bossed around. A handful of humiliating images become a focal point for something much bigger than themselves.

This at least helps to explain if not condone some of the violent protests in some Muslim cities and the language of some of the initial protesters in places like Copenhagen and London. Such behaviour is wholly un-acceptable and does great damage to the cause of the protesters and to the standing of Muslims in general. While violent protests do not win Muslims many friends, they are not the principal reason for a lack of sympathy for Muslims. Much more real estate has been burnt and more lives lost and endangered in protests in, say, Detroit or Los Angeles; in cases like that protest has been understood by many commentators and politicians as legitimate rage to be addressed by positive socio-economic policies.

Two factors are critical to the lack of sympathy for Muslims in Europe. Firstly, there is a lack of recognition that the way that Muslims are treated is a form of racism – after all its less than 15 years ago that the British Commission for Racial Equality and most British anti-racists denied that the vilification of Muslims was a form of racism. Most of continental Europe has hardly begun to have that debate. The sug-gestion that Muslims are not the subject of racism because they are a religious group is a nonsense when one considers that the victimisation of another religious group, the Jews, is paradigmatic of many people's understanding of racism, especially on the continent.

The second reason is the idea – prevalent amongst anti-racists, the pro-gressive intelligentsia and beyond – that religious people are not worthy of protection; more than that, they should be subject to not just intel-lectual criticism but mockery and ridicule.

The idea is that religion represents Europe's pre-enlightenment dark age of superstition and clerical authoritarianism and so has to be con-stantly kept at bay. Look at how Richard Dawkins in the recent BBC tele-vision series, *The Root of all Evil*, traduces faith by identifying all reli-gious people with the worst cases.

This understanding of religion is deep in the culture of the centre-left intelligentsia and is what is being appealed to in the current sloganeering around 'freedom of expression'. That's why when Muslims counter by citing what are regarded by Europeans as acceptable limits to freedom of speech (eg the imprisonment of Holocaust deniers), it cuts little ice for no one actually disagrees with limits to freedom of expression as such. It's just that some will not limit it in the field of religion. In this, liberals are no less following a creed, indeed are no less fundamentalist, than some of those who they want to be free to abuse.

Marginal or Equal?

Satirising clericalism may have been emancipatory but vilifying the marginal and exhorting integration is a contradiction. For radical secularism – no less than aspects of the 'this is our country, you Muslims will have to put up with our ways' right-wing nationalism – is an obstacle to Muslims becoming included in Europe and coming to have a sense of being part of Europe.

Europe is having to choose which is more important, the right to ridicule Muslims or the integration of Muslims. If the Danish cartoons have not been re-printed in Britain its because we came to this fork in the road with the *Satanic Verses* Affair. While we could not be said to have made a decisive choice there is greater understanding in Britain about anti-Muslim racism and about the vilification-integration contradiction than amongst some other European countries.

This is not to say that Muslim sensibilities must be treated as fixed. They too will rightly change and adapt to new contexts. The point is that this cannot be a one-way process. Civic integration and international interdependence – let alone anything as ambitious as a dialogue of civilisations – means that there has to be mutual learning and movement on both/all sides, not just the hurling of absolutes at each other. This is not just a matter of compromise but of multicultural inclusion: Muslim sensibilities, concerns and agendas should be knitted into society just as is the case when other marginalised groups or classes are accepted as democratic equals.

The current temper of the controversy in Britain – in particular the non-publication of the cartoons – is a sign of some progress since the *Satanic*

Verses Affair. But we have only just begun on a long journey and the task of carrying our EU partners with us makes it more uphill. The important thing is not to lose focus. If the goal is multicultural integration, then we must curb anti-Muslim racism and exercise restraint in the uses of freedom directed against religious people – who, after all, are a minority in Europe. Whilst in the US the Christian Right stand in the way of civic integration, the secularist intelligentsia needs to consider whether it is not playing the same role on our continent.

Note

1 For a critical discussion of this chapter and a reply, see T. Modood, R. Hansen, E. Bleich, B. O'Leary and J. Carens, 'The Danish Cartoon Affair: Free Speech, Racism, Islamism and Integration', *International Migration*, 44(5), 2006:p3-57)

5

Multicultural Citizenship and the Anti-Sharia Storm

From *Open Democracy* website, 14 February, 2008[1]

An intense public debate and media controversy was triggered in Britain after a lecture delivered by the Archbishop of Canterbury – the spiritual head of the Church of England – on 7 February 2008. The speech, 'Civil and Religious Law in England: a Religious Perspective'[1], raised important questions of law, state, faith and citizenship in a modern, plural society; and its bitter, polarising aftermath equally highlights the issue of what kind of civic discourse about these questions is necessary if they are to be properly addressed. This essay responds to the debate and controversy by viewing them in the perspective of 'multicultural citizenship', a concept which allows for nuanced understanding of the inter-relationship of 'secular' and 'religious' notions in civic life.

Rowan Williams's careful address explored the 'growing challenge' presented by 'the presence of communities which, while no less 'law-abiding' than the rest of the population, relate to something other than the British legal system alone', raised the question of 'what degree of accommodation the law of the land can and should give to minority communities with their own strongly entrenched legal and moral codes'; and included a developed and highly sensitive reflection on the reality and potential of 'plural jurisdiction', particularly in relation to the experience of and discussions about sharia courts, their capacity to rule on such matters as family disputes and claims, and their relationship to the 'statutory law of the United Kingdom'.

It may seem astonishing that a lecture at the Royal Courts of Justice in London, academic both in atmospherics and language, should generate such passionate denunciation. It is less so if seen in a context where the 'legal recognition of communal religious identities' conjures the worst suspicions and prejudices of those already attuned by a hostile public discourse to regard Islam-based practices, codes or ideas as by definition extreme or dangerous. Such sentiments are reinforced by a situation where criticism of multiculturalism – often focusing on its alleged socially divisive tendencies and supposed empowerment of reactionary religious forces – has become both routine and (often) ill-informed. In turn they fuel the argument that a turn towards a more or less rigorous secularism that would exclude recognition of religion in the public sphere is desirable. This line of argument, however, offers a false diagnosis and therefore a flawed prescription.

A particularly stark vision of these alternative social models was presented by David Hayes in the weeks after the terrorist attacks in London on 7 July 2005: the attacks, he argued, opened a new period in Britain's development where the choice was between 'radical multiculturalism' and 'radical secularism' (Hayes, 2005). But these are not our only choices, indeed they are not realistic choices because there is a deep resonance between citizenship and multicultural recognition. Not only do both presuppose complementary notions of unity and plurality, and of equality and difference, but the idea of respect for the group self-identities that citizens value is central to citizenship. This is the context, I suggest, within which this latest multiculturalism versus secularism storm should be understood.

Citizenship and Multicultural Citizenship
Multicultural citizenship is based on the idea that citizens have individual rights, but as individuals are not uniform, their citizenship contours itself around them. Citizenship is not a monistic identity that is completely apart from or transcends other identities important to citizens. Their group identities are ever present and each group has a right to be a part of the civic whole and to speak up for itself and for its vision of the whole.

Hence citizenship is a continuous dialogue. As the parties to these dialogues are many, not just two, the process may be described as multilogical. The multilogues allow for views to qualify each other, overlap, synthesise, modify one's own view in the light of having to co-exist with that of others, hybridise, allow new adjustments to be made, new conversations to take place. Such modulations and contestations are part of the internal, evolutionary, work-in-progress dynamic of citizenship. Thus, civic inclusion does not consist of an uncritical acceptance of an existing conception of citizenship, of 'the rules of the game" and a one-sided 'fitting-in' of new entrants (or the new equals – mostly ex-subordinates of the colonial experience). To be a citizen, no less than to have just become a citizen, is to have a right to not just be recognised but to debate the terms of recognition.

Citizenship consists of a number of coterminous processes: framework of rights and practices of participation; discourses and symbols of belonging, ways of imagining and remaking ourselves as a country and expressing our sense of commonalities; differences in ways in which these identities qualify each other and create inclusive public spaces. Change and reform do not all have to be brought about by state action, laws, regulation or prohibitions; they are also the result of public debate, discursive contestations, pressure group mobilisations, and the varied and (semi-) autonomous institutions of civil society.

Citizenship, then, is not confined to the state but dispersed across society, compatible with the multiple forms of contemporary groupness. It is sustained through dialogue, new and reformed national identities, plural forms of representation that do not take one group as the model to whom all others have to conform (Modood, 2007).

The ideal of multicultural citizenship is a critique of the cultural assimilation traditionally demanded by nation-states of migrants and minorities, as well as of that liberal individualism that has no space for groups. Nevertheless, it is clearly grounded in and is a development out of the ideas of individual equality and democratic citizenship. It is not about pre-democratic arrangements such as the Ottoman accommodation of minorities through the *millet* system. It seeks to pluralise, and hence adapt not undermine, the unity and equality of citizenship and national identity.

Multicultural Citizenship and Religion

What implications does this have for religious groups? It means that secularism *simpliciter* – the absolute and dogmatic separation of citizenship and religion – appear to be an obstacle to pluralistic integration and equality. This is a big implication but not as radical as it sounds. For secularism pure and simple is not what exists in Britain or indeed in any democratic country. Britain indeed is a secular country, a version of secularism is hegemonic; but it is of a moderate kind that accommodates organised religion, religious identities and conscience. This is evident in many areas: constitutional arrangements, schools, government support for welfare by religious agencies, Ministerial consultations with religious groups among them. These arrangements reflect a particular history to the point of idiosyncrasy but moderate secularism is the secularism of all democracies (rather than say Soviet Russia or Communist China) – even though each draws the religion-politics linkages and separations in its own way, as discussed in chapter 3 and further elaborated in chapter 11.

Given that multicultural citizenship is not narrowly defined in relation to the state but also to the varied areas of civil society and local government that shape and make meaningful our civic identities. It means that a focus on legal provisions is not the beginning or end of multicultural citizenship. But it is an important area, and so everything that the Archbishop of Canterbury said about the need to explore accommodating aspects of Muslim principles and laws (the heterogeneous collection of texts and forms of reasoning summed up as sharia) within United Kingdom law is relevant to the task of multiculturalising citizenship. The Archbishop was thinking about how the work of the existing Sharia Councils (which adjudicate on personal and civil matters such as divorce) could be extended and given legal recognition in the way that their Jewish equivalents have enjoyed for decades or longer.

He was quite clear that this was not a matter of separate or parallel legal systems for the *sharia* tribunals would not be able to go against UK laws, both on specifics such as for example divorce but also on individual and human rights in general. The decision to go to such Muslim adjudication services has of course to be voluntary by both parties, and above all the Archbishop rightly emphasised the importance of gender equality in these contexts. These courts would not have the power to punish or fine individuals and so they concern only civil matters, and have nothing to do with criminal justice.

Many people (wilfully or otherwise) misunderstood Archbishop Rowan's position and thought (sincerely or otherwise) that he was sanctioning the stoning of adulterers, hands-chopping for theft and beheadings for apostasy. Even some of those who recognise that he was not doing so still argue that his intentions here are not relevant, for by granting anything to Muslims in this regard would encourage extremists and unreasonable demands and propel the entire society down a slippery slope to a Talibanisation of British law.

This is scare-mongering on a large scale. To avoid discussing and conceding what is reasonable because someone else might later demand something unreasonable is irrational. And to associate a whole group, in this case Muslims, with their extremist elements is a kind of political demonisation that may appropriately be called anti-Muslim racism. Of course some Muslims may, just as anybody may, make unreasonable demands; but to therefore dismiss all Muslim demands is surely to draw the line between what is acceptable and unacceptable in the wrong place. As a matter of principle, each proposal should be considered on its own merits, and there is also wisdom in discussing and implementing proposals on a gradual basis so that their practical effects can be seen and lessons can be learned.

Legal Positivism and Critical Interpretivism

This is not just a matter of pragmatism and practical wisdom. It flows out of the ethics of multicultural citizenship: the imperative to seek the inclusion of marginal groups through dialogue, a commitment to seek mutual understanding and find accommodation. There is a yet deeper philosophical basis for what I am advocating. We should not ideologise *sharia* and secular law into rival, exclusive and inflexible systems. They have much in common both at the level of principles as well the capacity to live together. Those who think the opposite are likely to be influenced by a form of reasoning I will call legal positivism.

Positivists understand principles, bodies of thought and practice, traditions and so on as if they were self-evident and once learned all that is needed is to apply them in a legalistic way to a specific situation. Legal reasoning itself highlights the distortion of reasoning this embodies. For laws are not self-evident; otherwise why are there enormous legal libraries that contain voluminous commentaries, analyses and interpretations, as well as stacks of case law and precedent?

Interpretation and sensitivity to context are always essential to the application of a rule or law to a specific case. Understanding the rule depends upon reading it with other rules and principles which illuminate and qualify it. These rules and principles are not self-evident but rationally provoke questions which have to be critically engaged with. Understanding the situation to which the rule has to be applied requires the capacity to not just identify what is similar in that situation to all the other cases to which the rule applies, but also what is distinctive or new about the context and which may require us to question and refine the relevant body of principles and rules. In short, it requires the critical reasoning that Muslim jurists call *ijtihad*.

A simple illustration lies in the fact that at the time of the founding texts of Islam, there was no tobacco in Muslim societies. Hence the question of what attitude a believer should take to tobacco – to its cultivation, trade and consumption – is a matter of identifying the relevant rules and principles and showing in what ways and to what extent and under what conditions they apply to tobacco. To do that is to critically interrogate the texts and to extend the structure of thought and practice built upon them. In the process we end up not simply reflecting on a new case but may come to a new understanding of the principles, their inter-relationships, ambivalences, contradictions and so on and may come to reinterpret what was before thought to be settled. Some principles may thus be tightened and given greater definition, others loosened to widen their range of applicability and there can thus be implications for other cases and questions of behaviour.

Practical Multiculturalism

There are significant practical difficulties in giving public recognition and legal incorporation of sharia councils. They must of course work within United Kingdom law, only delivering judgements that are consistent with it, including human rights, gender equality and child protection legislation. There must be no compulsion or social pressure to go to them in preference to civil courts or other lawful remedies. The adjudicators need to be properly trained and qualified, both in terms of Islamic knowledge and authority but also in terms of their understanding of UK law and British society, the complex context in which the cases arise and within which they must be understood and resolved.

As there is no single ecclesiastical authority in Islam, certainly not in Sunni Islam, these problems cannot be addressed simply at the top and filtered down through a hierarchy. Yet it is a fact that *sharia* adjudication councils exist and operate in Britain and so it is very likely that some of the problems just mentioned are problems that already exist. These must be addressed but in sensitive and feasible ways; that is, not by picking a fight with Muslims but by bringing them deeper into British institutions and practice, and by equitable treatment that extends to Muslims the opportunities and resources that other groups enjoy.

This has some parallel with that of faith schools. In England there are thousands of Christian and some Jewish schools, largely funded by the public purse and which teach about a quarter of all pupils. So, when some private Muslim schools sought to enter this voluntary-aided sector their inclusion was reasonable and just and an appropriate elaboration of multicultural citizenship. But the process was neither simple nor automatic. The schools had to teach within a national curriculum, have competent teachers, appropriate facilities and governance, meet a local need and be open to professional inspection. Some private Muslim schools have been able to meet these criteria – indeed they meet them better than many comprehensives; others are working to reach these standards and most are outside the system.

This is a good model for how we can respond to the fact of the existence of shariah adjudication panels. We should accept the principle of their incorporation as a feature of our developing multicultural citizenship. We should use the existence of comparable Christian and Jewish institutions, such as the Beth Din, as a benchmark – though not inflexibly nor as a perfect model – and then consider the issues practically, including the safeguarding of individual rights, especially those of women and children, and look at each application on its own merits. Some applications may not be able to meet the requisite standards, others may not seek this formalisation (though that is not to say that they should be beyond all regulation and support if there was a cause for concern). We should proceed on a trial and error basis for while existing arrangements are a guide, so we are not wondering into the dark without any precedents, it is clear that some institutional innovation is likely to emerge and so, as always, caution is needed. Not only would this be a pragmatic way to proceed but it would be an appropriately British form of multicultural integration, something that works with the grain of what already exists (just as other countries may want to do it their own way too).

The storm that the Archbishop's views have provoked is in many ways more instructive than what he himself said. The reaction was immediate and has been wholly disproportionate. Part of the problem is language. Simply to say something positive about *sharia* leads to knee-jerk hostility amongst many people, just as the term 'secularism' regrettably is understood by some Muslims and others as a policy of atheism, colonialism and postcolonial despotism. The use of either of these terms can simply lead to the closing of minds, however reasonable and qualified is what is being said.

Beyond this, it is clearly indicative of deep insecurities and fears about Islam amongst many, probably most of our fellow citizens[2]. While this demonises and victimises us Muslims, the ethic of dialogical citizenship gives us a basis to both stand up for our equal status in a dignified way and to seek to address these fears sensitively and in the spirit of mutual concern and solidarity. It is not easy to be sympathetic and considerate when one is being attacked but our shared future depends upon handling even Islamophobic hysteria in the spirit of common citizenship. Britain belongs equally to all its citizens, its problems no less than its gifts. In mutual recognition of this shared ownership lies the hope of a secure and inclusive future.

Note

1 Available at <http://www.archbishopofcanterbury.org/1575>

2 For an analysis of a similar 'storm' in relation to the face veil, see Meer, Dwyer and Modood (2010)

6

Ethnicity, Muslims and Higher Education Entry in Britain

In *Teaching in Higher Education*, 2006[1]

I t is unfortunate that for many academics and educationalists ethnic minorities in Britain continue to be more associated with educational underachievement than success. This is specially reinforced when it comes to Muslims and especially Muslim men, about whom there is so much fear and demonisation at the moment. The latter is not just to do with terrorism but also about religious fanaticism and closed, inward-looking communities. These associations are a very partial – in both senses of the word – picture of how things actually are. Moreover, there are real questions of bias in the selection of university entrants.

Higher education in fact is a major success story for non-white ethnic minorities. This has been apparent since university entry data recorded ethnicity in 1990 (data is not recorded by religious affiliation) though it has not greatly disturbed sociological analyses that assume non-whiteness ('race') means educational underachievement (Modood, 2005).

A manifestation of this success is the achievement of entry into higher education. A few years ago the government set itself the target of getting 50 per cent of young people into higher education by the age of 30. Table 1 shows the state of play by ethnicity. It shows that by the year, 2001-2002, the likelihood of whites entering higher education was only 38 per cent and this was not just much lower than that of the ethnic

Table 1: Higher Education Initial Participation Rates (HEIPRs)
For England, ft and pt, 2001-02

Ethnic Group	Male	Female	All
White	34	41	38
All minority ethnic groups	55	58	56
Black Caribbean	36	52	45
Black African	71	75	73
Black Other	56	72	64
Indian	70	72	71
Pakistani	54	44	49
Bangladeshi	43	33	39
Chinese	47	50	49
Asian Other	74	94	83
Mixed ethnic	35	44	40
All (known ethnicity)	37	43	40

Source: Connor et al (2004)

minorities taken together but also lower than every single minority group. Sometimes it was not much lower (cf the Bangladeshis and the Black Caribbeans) and sometimes it was nearly half as low (cf the Black Africans and the Indians).[2]

So we have the extraordinary situation in Britain where white people are far from achieving the government target but all the minority groups except two have very nearly achieved it or greatly exceed it. Indeed ethnic minorities now represent almost one in six of home undergraduates in England, almost double their share of the population.

So this is a real achievement of ethnic minority families. One has to add, however, that this is not the full picture. Not only are there very significant differences between minority groups as we have already seen but ethnic minorities are less likely to enter the more prestigious universities, are more likely to drop out and if they last the course they are less likely to get a high grade degree (though all these things are less true of the Indians and the Chinese than of the other groups). Moreover, black groups are more likely to be part-time or mature students – qualities that do not produce the kind of high-flying careers that some associate with graduate status. Moreover, ethnic minorities are very unevenly distributed across subjects. They are disproportionally in medicine and health related subjects, law and business, engineering and ICT but are under-represented in the pure sciences and the humanities. So only a few universities and not all disciplines can truly claim to be multiethnic.

The causes of such disparities are due to many factors – students' pre-entry attainment levels, education choices at 16, subject preferences, geographical distribution, and aspirations are all key ingredients and all worth discussing. I would just like to discuss two factors, socio-economic class and institutional filtering.

Socio-economic class is a strong factor in a determining who gets where; for the white population it is a strong predictor of educational outcomes. For example, two-thirds of white students come from non-manual backgrounds. But class does not always work in the same way for ethnic minorities. Two-thirds of Pakistani and Bangladeshi students (nearly all of whom are from Muslim families) come from homes where the parents are in manual work or unemployed. One consequence of this is that while, as Table 1 shows, Pakistanis and Bangladeshis, are among the less successful of ethnic minority groups (and indeed are disproportionately in the less selective institutions and subjects) they are doing much better than their white working class peers, some of whom are not likely to be in university at all.

Nevertheless, when all the main factors are controlled for, there has been shown to be a bias against ethnic minorities in the pre-1992 universities and in their favour in the new universities (Shiner and Modood, 2002). Table 2 shows the probability of an offer to candidates with identical attainment scores, type of school background, age, gender, parental occupation etc and applying to the same course in the same type of institution. It reveals that even when all these things are controlled for there are ethnic biases in the likelihood of a university offering a place to a candidate. These biases vary across groups and are radically different across universities.

If we divide Britain's hundred-plus universities into those that have always been universities ('old universities') and those that were poly-technics till 1992 ('new universities', which are less wealthy and less

Table 2: Institutional 'Bias'
Rates of Success/Universities' Pecking Order

Old universities	New universities
Most preferred: Whites (0.75)*	*Most preferred:* Indians (0.85) Chinese (0.83) Bangladeshis (0.82)
Less preferred: Chinese (0.68) Black Caribbeans (0.65)	Less preferred: Pakistanis (0.77) Black Africans (0.76) Black Caribbeans (0.75) Whites (0.73)
Least preferred: Indian (0.58) Bangladeshis (0.57) Black Africans (0.57) Pakistanis (0.57)	

*Probability of initial offer to identical candidates for equivalent courses
Source: Shiner and Modood (2002)

selective than the old), we see that in the former, whites are more likely to get an offer than other identical candidates. For example, while a white student has a 75 per cent chance of an invitation to study, a Pakistani candidate, identical in every way, has only a 57 per cent chance of an offer. In the new universities, however, ethnic minorities are actually preferred though the scale of bias is less[3]. British universities, then, clearly need to review their methods of selection to identify and eliminate the sources of these biases.

It should be noted that about a third of non-whites in the UK are Muslim (though most Middle Easterners identify themselves as white). About two-thirds of Muslims are of South Asian origin, mostly Pakistanis. By most socio-economic measures Asian Muslims are amongst the most disadvantaged of the ethnic minorities. For example, over 60 per cent of Pakistani and Bangladeshi households are in poverty – compared to 20 per cent of whites – and have the highest proportions of school leavers without any qualifications[4]. Even that solid proportion of these two groups that are entering higher education are most likely to be in the less resourced institutions. Nevertheless, what the above analysis shows is that there is and continues to be a large scale familial and personal investment in education and a determination to achieve social mobility by means of higher education (Modood, 2004).

Interestingly, qualitative studies, including one I worked on with colleagues, suggest that for many young Asians Islam is appealed to – both by girls and boys – as a source of educational aspirations and the motivation to improve oneself and lead a disciplined, responsible life (Shah, Dwyer and Modood forthcoming). It is particularly used by girls to justify and negotiate educational and career opportunities with conservative parents, often of rural backgrounds with little knowledge of the scriptures; and by boys to distance themselves from the temptations of street youth culture, a primary obstacle to an academic pathway. Those boys who do not follow academic paths are not less but more likely to be assimilated into white working class lifestyles.

Hence, we must be careful in making any generalisations about Muslim cultures encouraging separatism, incapable of motivating youngsters to aspire to horizons beyond the ghetto or failing to encourage participation in British institutions. Islam in Britain is finely poised between a religion of a ghetto and a religion of social mobility – a kind of 'Protestant ethic' – capable of sustaining the hope and discipline that the taking up of opportunities requires. For the latter trajectory to be actualised, mainstream Islam requires encouragement not demonisation.

Notes

1 From: *Teaching in Higher Education*, 11 (2): 247-250, 2006, with kind permission of Taylor and Francis.

2 Not to mention the 'Asian Other', a term which includes disparate groups such as Sri Lankans, Vietnamese, Malayasians but which are relatively small in absolute terms and so working out the proportion of the age group in higher education is less reliable. The same may apply to the Chinese in Table 1 for their representation is much lower than all other data has suggested so far (see Modood, 2005).

3 Gittoes and Thompson (2007) reanalysed the same data by introducing some interactions and concluded that 'ethnic minorities are not treated more or less favourably in the application process by different types of institution' (423). Nevertheless they too found Pakistani applicants had a lower than expected offer rate across the whole higher

education sector and applicants from all ethnic minority groups, apart from Chinese, had lower than expected offer rates when applying to study law. They suggested therefore that UCAS should 'withhold applicants' names for the first stages of the application process' (423). Michael Shiner and Philip Noden at the LSE are currently leading a project to further analyse UCAS data to identify what factors are driving differential patterns of entry, with the aim of publishing results in 2011.

4 For the latest data, systematically analysed not just in relation to ethnicity and religious groups but also to a wide range of cross-cutting and structural dimensions, see NEP 2010.

7

British Muslim Perspectives on Multiculturalism

with Fauzia Ahmad

From *Theory, Culture and Society*, March 2007[1]

There is a general understanding today that Britain is a multicultural society but what does this mean, how effective is it in practice and what questions does it raise about institutional racism, citizenship and national identity? Can we, in the current lexicon of the UK Home Office, talk with any coherence about 'cohesive communities'? How are these defined – by 'race', ethnicity, national origins or religion?

The characterisation of post-migration relations in Britain, at least till the late 1980s was premised on the idea that 'colour-racism' defined the relationship, that it was a black-white racial dualism. With the splintering of 'black' into 'black and Asian' and later, the rise of religious identities like Sikh and Muslim, a more pluralistic situation developed. With increasing evidence that South Asians, especially Muslims, give religion rather than national origins a greater salience in self-concepts and an on-going series of political crises featuring Muslims rather than Asians or non-whites *per se*, from the Rushdie Affair in 1988-89 to the first Gulf war in 1991, the controversies around Muslim faith schools, September 11, the resulting wars in Afghanistan and Iraq and the 7/7 bombings, the term 'Asian' has ceased to have much content as a political category. It still has some resonance as a self-identity for some, especially young people, mainly in relation to a new, hybrid British Asian culture, but it is 'Muslim' that has emerged as the most prominent and charged communal category. Demography also has some relevance here, for at 1.5 million in the 2001 Census, Muslims are as numerous as all other non-Christian minority faiths. (They also constitute more than a third of non-whites, though this estimation is complicated by the fact that most Middle Easterners regard themselves as white, though it is doubtful that others unambiguously regard them as such.) Thus new questions have been raised about tolerance and the conformity that a dominant culture which aspires to be liberal, democratic and inclusive may require from minority cultures and whether we need a new extended concept of racism which can incorporate the hostility against Muslims; and about the place of religion in the political culture and institutions.

All these questions, which are central to working out a viable multiculturalism in Britain, were thrown into sharp relief by September 11 and its aftermath. There have been many reports of harassment and attacks against Muslims, and Muslims, who have expressed both vulnerability and defiance, have become a focus of national concern and debate. Muslim Britons have found themselves bearing the brunt of a new wave of suspicion and hostility, and strongly voiced if imprecise doubts have been cast on their loyalty as citizens (Werbner, 2001). There has been wide-spread questioning about whether Muslims can be and are willing to be integrated into British society and its political values. This has ranged from anxiety about terrorist cells and networks recruiting alienated young Muslims for mischief abroad and as a 'fifth column' at home; to whether Muslims are willing to give loyalty to the British state rather than to transnational Muslim leaders and causes; and to whether Muslims are committed to what are taken to be the core British values of freedom, tolerance, democracy, sexual equality and secularism. Many politicians, commentators, letter-writers and phone-callers to the media from across the political spectrum, not to mention Home Secretaries, have blamed the fact that these questions have had to be asked on the alleged cultural separatism and self-imposed segregation of Muslim migrants and on a 'politically correct' concept of multiculturalism that had fostered fragmentation rather than integration and 'Britishness' (*The Independent on Sunday*, 9 December 2001).

There is also a further problem in relation to Muslims and religious minorities and current political attacks on multiculturalism (for elaboration of the argument below, see Modood 2005). When the term 'multiculturalism' emerged in the 1970s in Britain the initial policy focus was primarily on schooling. Multiculturalism meant the extension of the school, both in terms of curriculum and as an institution, to include features such as 'mother-tongue' teaching, black history, Asian dress and – importantly – non-Christian religions and holidays, religious dietary requirements and so on. It was criticised by socialists and antiracists as not focusing on the real social divisions and causes of inequality and caricatured as a preoccupation with 'saris, steel bands and samosas' (Troyna, 1987 and 1993, Modood and May, 2001). One consequence was a perhaps unnecessary and prolonged division between antiracists and multiculturalists; another was that religious identity issues were marginalised even by advocates of multicultural education (Swann, 1985). Relatedly, as anti-discrimination legislation and policies were developed in Britain, the initial focus was on colour-racism. After a cursory discussion in Parliament, an amendment to include religion as a ground of discrimination in the 1976 Race Relations Act was withdrawn. However, while the Jews were taken to be a 'race' by the legislators and the courts, and the *Mandala* decision of the House of Lords judges in 1982 included another ethno-religious community, the Sikhs, within the protection of the Act, Muslims were judged to be solely a religious group and so direct discrimination against them was lawful (except in N. Ireland) till the end of 2003, when religious discrimination in employment was made an offence.

This marginality of religious identity in the British equalities framework is a reflection of the wider culture in which it seemed reasonable to simultaneously argue against colour-blindness and in favour of racial explicitness in policy; to celebrate and promote respect for black and ethnic minority identities; to argue that marginalised identities needed to be brought from the margins to the centre of public identity formation; and at the same time to argue that religion was a matter not of mutual respect but of mutual tolerance and had to be confined to a private sphere. This dichotomy between race/ethnicity on the one hand, and religion on the other, became part of the foundations of the theories of multiculturalism and politics of 'difference' as they came to be elaborated in the 1980s and 1990s. For example, Will Kymlicka, the leading international liberal theorist of multiculturalism, argues that a strict separation of state and ethnicity is incoherent but is content to apply the separation model to religion (Kymlicka, 1995:107-108; 2001: 24; Modood, 2007). Similarly, the feminist political philosopher, Iris Young, develops a theory of empowerment for all forms of marginal groups (critics have joked that her amalgam of minorities includes eighty per cent of the population for it only seems to leave out able-bodied, heterosexual white males) without mentioning religion, which does not even feature as a term in the index (Young, 1990; for a later contrast, see Parekh, 2000). In theory and in practice, then, while minority racial and ethnic assertiveness (not to mention women's movements and gay pride) were encouraged by egalitarians, religious assertiveness, especially Muslim – when it occurred – was seen as a problem; not as a strand within equality struggles but as a threat to multiculturalism. The *Satanic Verses* Affair at the end of the 1980s is a notable example: it horrified liberals and socialists alike and divided both multiculturalists and anti-racists. An instance of which is that it led the Southall Black Sisters to found 'Women Against Fundamentalism' to oppose the Muslim protesters against the novel (WAF, 1990; Yuval-Davis, 1992).

All these tensions have grown and in the aftermath of 9/11 and 7/7 seem to be set to grow further. They are not necessarily irresolvable but the tension between Muslim assertiveness (in its varying forms) and the deeply embedded secularism of most liberal democracies is at the heart of what is perceived as a 'crisis of multiculturalism' in most of the countries of western Europe (Modood *et al*, 2006 and Modood, 2007).

The Role of 'Moderate' Muslims

One of the interesting aspects about the post 9/11 public statements of Muslims, which for example was missing at the time of the protests against Salman Rushdie's novel, *The Satanic Verses*, is the expression of self-criticism. Some Muslim commentators writing in the non-Muslim media, while maintaining a strongly anti-US/Western foreign policy stance, have expressed shock at how much anger and latent violence has become part of British Muslim, especially youth, culture, arguing that West-hating militant ideologues had 'hijacked' Islam and that the 'moderates' had to denounce them.[2] The following quote from Yusuf Islam, the head of the Islamia Educational Trust, nicely captures this shift in the position of the 'moderates':

> [At the time of the Rushdie Affair] I was still learning, ill-prepared and lacking in knowledge and confidence to speak out against forms of extremism... Today, I am aghast at the horror of recent events and feel it a duty to speak out. Not only did terrorists hijack planes and destroy life, they also hijacked the beautiful religion of Islam. (*The Independent*, 26 October, 2001)

Some Muslim intellectuals issued 'fatwas' against the fanatics (Ziauddin Sardar, *The Observer*, 23 September, 2001), and described the Muslim revolutionaries as 'fascists' (Sardar, *Evening Standard*, 5 November, 2001) and 'xenophobes' (Yasmin Alibhai-Brown, *The Independent*, 5 November, 2001), with whom they did not want to be united in the term 'British Muslims'[3]. While in the *Satanic Verses* Affair 'moderate' Muslims argued against what they took to be a bias against Muslims – a failure even by liberals to extend the ideas of equality and respect for others to include Muslims – to this line of defence 'moderates' now added a discourse about the urgency of reinterpreting or re-reading Islam in an effort to retrieve and revive notions of tolerance, equality and compassion. This is variously taken to be a re-excavation of the Qur'an as a charter of human rights, which, for example, abolished slavery and gave property rights to women more than a millennium before either of these was achieved in the West; a restoration of the thirst for knowledge and rational enquiry which characterised medieval Muslim societies; a re-centring of Islam around piety and spirituality, not political ideology; a 'reformation' that would make Islam compatible with individual conscience, science and secularism. Ziauddin Sardar, one of the most prominent of the 'moderate' Muslim intellectuals identified the failure of the Islamist movements of the 1960s and 1970s as among the causes of the contemporary distortions of political Islam. Such movements, he argued, had started off with an ethical and intellectual idealism but had become intellectually closed, fanatical and violent. As today's middle-aged moderates had encouraged the earlier Islamic renewal, they must now take some responsibility for what had come to pass and must do something about it (Sardar, *The Observer*, 21 October 2001). This aspect of self-criticism was also found in Muslim discourses following the London bombings on July 7, 2005[4].

Defining 'Moderate Muslims'

This chapter is based on a research project that sought to explore the perceptions of some key Muslims in Britain on the place of Muslims in the kind of multicultural society that Britain is becoming or could become. It was conceived with September 11 and its aftermath as a backdrop. This included the fear and anger that was being directed against Muslims for their real or imagined association with enemies of Britain, Islamic militancy and terrorism. The Muslims whose perceptions we researched were identified on the basis of two criteria. Firstly, they had to be 'public' figures – visibly active as intellectuals, commentators and/ or community activists or leaders engaged in debates about the politics of being Muslim in Britain. Some of them appear regularly on, say, current affairs television and in the opinion columns of the broadsheet newspapers, while others were less well known in the mainstream media but were prominent in Muslim community organisations and were regular speakers and contributors to Muslim public meetings, magazines and websites[5].

Secondly, they had to be 'moderate'. This is a difficult, indeed, controversial term, which as we discuss below was rejected by some of those who we interviewed. Nevertheless, despite difficulties of terminology, we clearly chose to interview Muslims who held one kind of view and not another kind of view. So, by 'moderate Muslim' here is meant Muslims who are anti-terrorism (whether in the name of Islam or otherwise) and who are opposed to the invocation of Islam in militant political rhetoric. More specifically, they are opposed to the 'clash of civilisations' thesis, as espoused by, for example, American neo-conservatives and radical Islamists (another potentially controversial term), which claims that Islam and the West are two monoliths that are at war with each other and that the war is inevitable and stems from a deep, civilisational difference and antagonism.

'Moderate Muslim' is obviously a relational term: it only makes sense in terms of a contrast with non-moderates, as is always the case in a moderate-radical couplet (*cf* moderate feminist and radical feminist). While the discourse of 'moderation' is most clearly a reaction to, and defined in opposition to terrorism of the kind that took place on 9/11, we can perhaps very briefly sketch the interpretation of Islam that on the whole 'moderation' is opposed to. As above, it must be stressed, however, that we are not claiming that all the individuals we refer to later in this chapter share this definition of 'non-moderation'. Nevertheless, we might find it useful to draw on the arguments presented by Omid Safi (2003) for the development of a 'progressive Muslim discourse' in opposition to a 'non-progressive' one. This involves openly challenging and resisting oppressive regimes and practices that promote violations of basic human rights such as freedom of expression as seen in several Muslim countries (for example, Saudi Arabia, Turkey, Pakistan, etc). It also involves challenging regimes such as the Taliban, that promote narrow interpretations of the Qur'an, as demonstrated in its extreme forms of gender segregation, or the persecution of ethnic and religious minorities. As Safi goes on to say, 'it means embracing and implementing a different vision of Islam than that offered by Wahhabi and neo-Wahhabi groups' whilst remaining careful to avoid 'de-humanising' and demonising those that profess Wahhabist leanings (2003:2). Besides rejecting certain versions of Islam, it also includes a strenuous resistance to 'hegemonic Western political, economic and intellectual structures that promote an unequal distribution of resources around the world' (2003:2).

In contrast, non-moderate Islam can be seen as ahistorical and making no concessions to interpretation and context. Actions that are prescribed in the Qur'an (eg compassionate treatment of slaves) are taken to be equally appropriate today, a time when slavery has no moral justification. Similarly, the harsh punishments of *hudod*, such as the cutting off of the hand of a thief, are read as if they apply to all times and places, without regard to levels of poverty and welfare and the achievement of social justice that the Qur'an exhorts. The Qur'an and Shariah are thus read as not primarily enunciating and illustrating principles for correct action but as concrete and fixed sets of actions. Prominent themes and principles within the Qur'an and re-iterated in Shariah and the Hadith such as mercy, compassion and social justice, are relegated to the background in favour of narrow, rigid interpretations and extreme actions. No room for critical reasoning and interpretation (*ijtihad*) is allowed but a particular dogmatic interpretation is asserted to be the only one possible. Added to this is a concept of 'jihad' in which military action – rather than spiritual, ethical or even political struggle – is given primacy and is seen as most apposite in the world today. It is this narrow, reductionist view of Islam and human conduct without a full understanding of the scope of Quranic teachings and principles, and a rejection of anything 'Western' that can be highly dangerous when directed towards political power or martyrdom. It is this rigid, fanatical (not to be confused with the term 'fundamentalist' – another contested term[6]) and exclusionist vision of Islam that 'a progressive' perspective denounces and opposes.

'Moderate Muslim' is a relational concept in another, deeper sense too. It is about a relationship between Muslims and the 'West'. Moderate Muslims in the British or any other Western context, seek, albeit in different ways, positive mutual interaction between things Western and things Islamic, including socio-political integration and self-integration, ie integrating aspects of one's thinking and behaviour which is Muslim and aspects of one's thinking and behaviour which is Western, so that there is no clear boundary or antagonism between the two (*cf* Roy, 2004). The idea of reconciling two sets of intellectual-practical commitments, holding on to one without rejecting the other but seeking to make compatible the best from both, and to do so as a form of politics is central to the concept of 'moderate Muslim'. So 'moderate Muslim' can be seen as an explicit and reasoned struggle to create a hybrid position. At least sociologically, it is more like a 'hyphenated identity' than an interpretation of the Qur'an, though of course the motive for it may come from the Qur'an and it may have to be justified by an appeal to Islamic texts and precedents. Nevertheless, the non-Muslim context can be critical too. Of particular pertinence here is the suggestion that British Muslim political activism in relation to domestic politics is an outgrowth of movements for racial equality and multiculturalism (Modood, 2002 and 2005).

One of the key distinctions between the 'Progressive Muslim' discourse in the US and those we interviewed is that whilst the former represents a collective of individuals (such as Farid Esack, Amina Wadud, Kecia Ali, Ahmad S Mousalli and Akbar S Ahmed to name a few) who openly identify as part of a 'movement', those in our sample do not. They speak as either individuals or as representatives (elected or otherwise) of groups and organisations and as such demonstrate a diverse range of Muslim experience, opinion and interests[7]. In any case, the important point to emphasise is that 'Moderate Muslim' is not a single position but refers to a broad and vibrant field of identity debates and positions. Moreover, in relation to both our criteria, 'Muslim' operated as a socio-logical category for identification, not as a faith category. For the purposes of our study it was sufficient that individuals selected were either actively a part of a Muslim community, group or organisation, perceived themselves as a Muslim, and/or were perceived by others as a Muslim.[8] (See Appendix 'A' for list of interviewees).

While our interviewees in our opinion conformed to these criteria, not all were happy with the term 'moderate'. Despite the recent claim that among Muslims it 'has actually become somewhat fashionable these days to refer to oneself or one's ilk as 'being a moderate' (Bokhari, 2004: 34), some of our respondents objected to the term in the title of the research project and we believe that it may even have influenced some to not co-operate. Of those who participated, several said that it was a divisive term, sorting Muslims into 'good' and 'bad' Muslims and so unhelpful, especially as it was external to Muslim discourses and seemed an invention of the Western media and politicians (Mamdani, 2002). Some objected that Islam, being the 'Middle Way', was already a religion of moderation and so did not need the prefix, 'moderate'. All said that the term had a negative association amongst some sections of the Muslim community which constrained its use. As it was a term used of and used by politicians, including leaders of some Muslim countries, who were seen to be uncritically supportive of Western interests and policies, it had come to be synonymous with terms such as 'stooge', 'collaborator' and 'sell-out'.[9] So much so, that even those who thought the term was reasonable and in some contexts would use it to describe themselves found themselves having to be cautious. Some of these multi-layered meanings are nicely caught in the following quote from Ghayasuddin Siddiqui, Leader of the 'Muslim Parliament':

> 'I'm reluctant to use this word, because it has come, as they call it, from non-Islamic sources, but I think we must hold the middle ground.'

A number of assumptions and implications can be identified in this quote:

i)   Islam is the middle ground which he remains firm about;

ii) He has nothing against the term 'moderate' but he is in a dilemma because:

a) Muslim extremists have fouled the term with their sneers and accusations and,

b) the term also has negative meanings within the wider British Muslim community as it implies a certain compromising of Islamic ideals.

iii) The term therefore cannot be safely used to mark and hold the middle ground.

As a result of the responses described above we gave considerable and prolonged thought to substituting the word 'moderate'. Despite consulting many people, we failed to come up with a term that equally adequately met our criteria, as expounded above. Terms such as 'mainstream', 'liberal', 'traditional', 'British' and others were offered but each was deemed by us to be less adequate, either because they were too extensive (eg 'mainstream', 'British') or too narrow ('traditional') or too contested ('liberal').[10] We believe therefore that two of the important findings of this project are the rejection of the term 'moderate' by so many of our respondents and others; and that no alternative term can be identified. We mark this dual finding by using the term 'moderate Muslim' in quote marks throughout.

As mentioned, we did not take 'moderate Muslim' to be a single position but a number of approaches (which could be overlapping) to expressing Muslim identities in contemporary Britain. For the purposes of this project we characterised some of the important positions we were interested in the following way:

1. '*Traditional Islam*'
Reasoning from faith and first principles but doing so in the way of the traditional ulemma or, more likely, in a way not opposed to traditional Islamic learning.

2. '*Modernist Islam*'
Reasoning from faith and first principles but doing so in ways which draw upon modernist ideas within an Islamic methodology (*Ijtihad*).

3. '*Philosophical Muslim*'
Reasoning from first principles but without much systematic reference to Islam and drawing more on modern Western theory, ethics and principles, including arguments about multiculturalism, equality and so on.

4. 'Existential Muslim'

Arguing in a more existential and pragmatic way, eg linking the communities and institutions that one belongs to, say, Muslims and the Labour Party, or Muslims and racial equality institutions. Or to treat being 'British Muslim' as a hyphenated identity in which both parts are to be valued as important to oneself and one's principles and belief commitments.

We sought to represent all four of these intellectual positions in selecting our sample. We did not expect to cover each equally and did not do so, with the first position proving to be the most covered, though of course individuals did not neatly fall into one way of thinking or another. Shadid and Van Koningsveld (1996) classify Islamic perspectives on Muslims living in non-Muslim countries into four on the basis of the position taken on the classical division of the world into a 'Territory of Islam' and 'Territory of War' (Shadid and Van Koningsveld, 1996). That classification had no purchase in our study as none of our interviewees made any reference to these classical concepts and therefore all of our respondents fall into only one of those four categories, namely, an implicit and pragmatic rejection of the classical division of the world into an oppositional 'Us' and 'Them'[11]. We would suggest that Shadid and Van Koningsveld's classification is only useful in relation to those who do not think of themselves as British (perhaps some non-naturalised 'first generation' immigrants) or radical Islamists – who by definition were not included in the study. Perhaps a more pertinent contrast with our four identified positions within the category 'moderate' or mainstream is with the eight offered by Saied Reza Ameli (2002) in his study of British born Muslims in the London Borough of Brent. Basing his typologies on the three forms of identity construction originally proposed by Castells (1997), Ameli distinguishes between eight differing but correlated types of British Muslim identity that reflect local, global and historical influences. He lists these as Nationalist, Traditional, Islamist, Modernised, Secular, Anglicised (Westernised), Hybrid, and Undetermined or 'disorganised' referring particularly to younger generations that display little loyalty to either their families' country of origin or Britain. Like our study, he sought to differentiate along sociological lines rather than religious ones, though of course he casts a much wider net than we do and, in contrast to Ameli, our categorisation was used to identify the sample and not as a tool of analysis or as a conclusion of research. With specific reference to those who refer to themselves as 'moderate' Muslims, Bokhari believes they can be sorted into 'moderate Islamists, traditional Muslims, liberal Muslims, and certain regimes in the Muslim world' (Bokhari, 2004:34). Interestingly, he suggests that 'the shunning of the use of force to promote a particularistic political agenda should be the minimum requirement to qualify as a moderate Muslim' and that the term should be about respecting the plurality of *ijtihad* (Bokhari, 2004:35).

Beyond specific exercises in categorisation, there are of course various studies of Muslim discourses in Britain and how they sometimes use British race relations discourses (eg Lewis, 1994; Werbner, 2002) or how young British Muslims interpret being Muslim and British (eg J. Jacobson 1997), and Muslim intellectual perspectives on the socio-political contexts of Muslims in the West (eg Ahmed, 2003). As far as we are aware, no previous study has attempted to empirically identify the positions of Muslim intellectuals and activists on multiculturalism and related concepts such as equality, citizenship and belonging. We do not attempt to locate the positions we discuss here to the philosophies of the nineteenth and twentieth century reformist Muslim intellectuals; rather, the conceptualisation used here to identify 'moderate Muslims' and different strands therein is original to this project.

Some will consider that our project as an inquiry into Muslim perspectives on multiculturalism is misconceptualised. They may contend that it should be framed as an inquiry into religious pluralism.[12] We, however, think that contemporary notions of multicultural equality and respect are a more appropriate discourse than the more traditional notions of religious pluralism and tolerance for understanding Muslim civic claims-making in contemporary Britain (Modood, 2007). Our invitation to our respondents was explicitly couched in terms of a request for an interview on a project on 'Moderate Muslims and the Politics of Multiculturalism'. While some, as we note below, queried the notion of multiculturalism, most were concerned to extend multiculturalism to encompass faith groups rather than to seek a domain of tolerance. We believe that both perspectives may be pertinent in their own way and each can benefit from mutual engagement.

Methodology

Interviews lasting an average of about two hours were undertaken during January-May 2003 in London. Our goal was twenty semi-structured interviews with prominent Muslims, though we achieved twenty-one. Four of our contributors were women. The interview schedule was piloted and each interview was tape-recorded and transcribed. The interviews, due to the nature of the debates and our prior personal relationships with interviewees, were at times, informal in nature and most can be said to have taken on the form of 'structured conversations'. Therefore, interviews were organic in that we allowed respondents to discuss issues they felt particularly passionate about or keen to elaborate upon, and allowed the interview to progress and develop as themes emerged. We did not need to keep to a rigid list of questions, as many respondents elaborated upon related items during the course of their responses and the discussion.

In addition, a number of key written articles were also referred to as part of the research process in helping us to map out the debates. Interviewees were invited to refer us to articles they felt relevant to the research questions and to add further comments on the research throughout the research process.

Multiculturalism as a Muslim Position

None of our interviewees argued against the ideal of multiculturalism. There were two main dimensions arising from the interviews regarding multiculturalism. One was the emphasis many placed on the inherent plurality in Islam, the Qur'an and Islamic history, as well as contemporary examples. The other was an evaluation of the realities of multiculturalism as manifested and practiced in Britain.

Islam as Inherently Multicultural

There were two main ways in which contributors highlighted Islamic perspectives and contributions to debates on multiculturalism. One was to refer to specific Qur'anic passages whilst the other was to refer to examples from Islamic history. For example, the writer, broadcaster and convert, Merryl Wyn-Davies cited the Qur'anic verse beginning, '*We have created you nations and tribes, that you may know one another*', and '*We have created colours and tongues*'. She linked these quotes to the concepts of identity and citizenship, arguing that Islam 'allows difference to flourish':

> The whole sense of identity – the Qur'an does not talk in the language of rights, rather the language of endowments and obligations and responsibilities – but if you wanted to say, the right to an identity, up to and including a different religious identity is guaranteed within the matrix of the Qur'an. The Qur'an is to me inherently multicultural.

Wyn-Davies has in fact devoted a book to the idea of pluralism in Islam (Wyn-Davies, 1988; see also Khan, 2002 and Asani, 2003 for 'ideas that form the seeds for a theology of pluralism within Islam'). Many other respondents referred to examples throughout Islamic history to illustrate how concepts of multiculturalism, or rather plurality, were enshrined and practiced within Islamic traditions of governance. For example, the late Sheikh Dr Zaki Badawi (not in our sample, but spoken to informally) has stressed that the constitution of Medina, under the Prophet Muhammad's leadership, was the first example of a multicultural constitution in history in that it guaranteed autonomy to the various communities of the city (Badawi, 2003). The Ottoman millat system is also often cited in contemporary discussions as a model of multiculturalism (Kymlicka, 1992; Modood, 1997). Similarly, contributors referred to the histories of Spain, India and the Middle East as examples of how tolerant and plural these societies were under Muslim rule, with faith communities being able to run their own affairs, as well as to dialogue with and learn from each other.

Although current political situations were often far removed from original Islamic influences, personal encounters and experiences with the Muslim world were illustrative of Muslim tolerance and respect for diversity. Documentary film-maker Navid Akhtar spoke of personal experiences and also referred to Islamic history:

> Wherever I've travelled in the world, I've seen how other societies, other communities work ... people can live in harmony and they have managed to do that and also throughout history we can see that there's been incredible tolerance when Muslims have actually had the upper hand, there's been immense tolerance and immense sense of respect for other religions, for non-Muslims, that's dictated by revelation in the Qur'an.

Malaysia, despite some of the serious problems of corruption and authoritarianism within Malay politics, was held by Wyn-Davies as an example of a contemporary Muslim state that represented an Islamic model of pluralism in action since its constitution encouraged the communal sharing of the diverse range of religious traditions and symbols across society. After having lived some years in Malaysia, she believed it to be:

> ... the only genuinely functioning, truly definitional multicultural society in the world. That multiculturalism is operated under a constitution where Islam is the state religion but all other communities, cultures and religions are guaranteed within the constitution and have a communal role in politics ... Everybody takes it in turn so that everybody has public presentation of their identity within the public space, and the sense of sharing that identity. Now that to me, I think is beyond multiculturalism. I think that is called genuine plurality.

Tolerance versus Mutual Acceptance and Mutual Respect

Islamic concepts of 'tolerance', as noted by Akhtar above, were contrasted with British debates where the question of 'tolerance' was contextualised differently. Shahid Malik (who was a Parliamentary candidate at the time and later became a Labour MP and then a government Minister), like some others, believed that 'tolerance' was 'fickle' and preferred instead to talk about 'mutual acceptance' as a more 'interactive' avenue through which respect for difference could emerge. For Muslims he felt this also meant accepting the rights of others who were different, such as gay groups, to co-exist with respect:

> ... we need something much more substantive and meaningful than [tolerance]. I suppose that's when mutual acceptance comes into it which is much deeper, its saying you're actually taking time out to understand where different people are coming from, you respect where they're coming from, and you understand it. (Shahid Malik)

However, though generally agreeing with the concept of respect for individuals, others within our sample were careful to distinguish between this and the religious and political acceptance of alternative forms of sexuality by Muslims, seeing that as contradictory to Islamic principles. For instance, Sir Iqbal Sacranie, at the time the General Secretary of the Muslim Council of Britain (MCB) strongly opposed moves to repeal 'Section 28' and so allow same-sex partnerships to be presented within school education as valid alternatives:

> ... [support for opposition to] Section 28 ... is totally alien to Islam ... we are making our position very clear that we cannot be a part of the liberal lobby ... that goes against the very principle of existence, so that's one area where we have to stick with the principles.

Similarly, Anas Altikriti, Press Spokesperson of the Muslim Association of Britain (MAB), which jointly led a number of successful anti-war marches and demonstrations by forming alliances with left-wing political movements, did not want to make a political issue of homosexuality:

> This issue we have decided not to touch on. As Muslims we're very clear on this, that these are wrong activities. However, we also have another principle of Islam, that is personal life-style, the personal tastes of an individual is up to them.

The issue of sexuality, then, is in fact one of the pivotal points of contention between secular liberals and 'mainstream', practising Muslims within Western multicultural societies, and among Muslims themselves. It, together with the wider theme of sexual freedom, is central to the political hostility against Muslims in, for example, the Netherlands, where the gay sociology professor, Pim Fortuyn, led a popular movement to restrict Muslim immigration because the attitudes of Muslims were alleged to be threatening traditional Dutch sexual liberalism. In London, when Mayor Ken Livingstone invited Shaikh al-Qaradawi (regarded by many Muslims as a moderate), who is based in Qatar but is the President of the European Council for Fatwa and Research, one of the foci of opposition to his visit was led by the gay rights group, Outrage.[13] Indeed, conceptually the issue is critical to the tensions between the idea of tolerating a disapproved lifestyle and the mutual acceptance of difference.

Muslims may not want simply to be tolerated but there are clearly groups to whom some Muslims cannot themselves extend more than toleration. The Islamic ideal of plurality that some of our respondents referred to is not just about tolerating other religious communities but respecting them and sharing the public space with them; it, however, cannot offer more than toleration for what cannot be respected within

Islam. The contemporary, secular, western discourse of multicultura-lism, on the other hand, seems to see all sexual orientations based on informed adult consent as equally worthy of respect and public space, but prefers to see religion as tolerated if confined to the private sphere (Modood, 2002). The two views are mirror-images of each other: in one homosexuality, in the other, religion, is tolerated as a private vice – like 'a dirty smell', as Shahid Malik put it – while other forms of difference are respected. Each distributes tolerance and respect differently but each employs a toleration/respect distinction.

This leads to not just different interpretations of multiculturalism but has the potential for policy conflicts. In Britain groups that mobilised on the basis of faith such as Muslims could, until recently, only access public resources if they complied with certain equal opportunities' frameworks that could potentially oblige them to share resources with gay organisations or employ openly gay individuals. In response, Muslim organisations have argued that in order to maintain their Islamic identities, compromise on the issue of sexuality, as now advo-cated by some within the Church of England, is unacceptable.

Celebration of Commonality

While most critiques of multiculturalism from our sample were directed towards its tendency to emphasise superficial differences in the name of cultural diversity, or its failure to engage with faith-based identities, some, such as Shahid Malik, also noted its failure to draw on shared commonalities across cultures:

> ... We celebrate diversity on occasions but we don't ever really *celebrate commonality* and the reality is that all these different cultures and religions that we speak of, actually 90 per cent of what they believe in is common to all of them, but we ignore the common and focus on that which isn't common. And actually if we firstly focused on that which is common, it would make the things that makes us different more digestible.

The issue of commonality was also raised by Sacranie, when explaining the development of Muslim organisations in the UK and how the MCB's motto 'Working for the Common Good', was designed to 'bring Islam in an inclusive way' by stressing that 'anything we do has to also benefit the wider community.' Commonality was most stressed by the franco-phone Swiss public intellectual, Tariq Ramadan, for some years a regular presence at British meetings and currently resident in Britain, who is strongly opposed to any kind of philosophical particularism and political communalism. He emphasised that citizenship was indivisible and that no one could be a 'minority citizen':

> Equal citizenship means that we have to go out from our intellectual and cultural ghettos. To come to the mainstream society and say 'ok, I am a British citizen, I am a French citizen'. To do that, we have to understand that there is no minority citizenship in this country... *as a citizen*, I am not part of a minority, I am a citizen, with my Islamic background and faith, but I am a citizen. And here is the link, between universal principles and considering yourself as being part of mainstream society. And this is main challenge of the years to come, and we have to build a concept of citizenship on that.

He cautioned against 'falling into the trap of the minority mind-set' as this compromised the establishment of universal values shared by both Muslims and non-Muslims. Ramadan further argued that the creation of a minority discourse was, in effect, a colonialist strategy that acted to prevent full integration and participation into mainstream society and equal citizenship. The challenge now was to build a concept of citizenship that facilitated the sharing of universal values. This was not only not inconsistent with being a Muslim but in fact the search for commonality was directly derived from the universalism of Islam, no less than from the universalism of western ethical traditions. In his philosophical writings Ramadan develops this distinctive position in which he derives a form of civic integrationism by an appeal to faith. While his starting point is Islam, it is one which, far from being anti-Western, affirms ethical universalism as a basis for being a European or Western Muslim, civic obligations and anti-relativism (Ramadan, 2004a; see also Bechler, 2004).[14]

Dialogue and Transformation of Minorities and Majorities

Many of the respondents emphasised the importance of dialogue. For example, the legal academic, Maleiha Malik, stressed that 'multiculturalism requires two-way compromise and its not just an effort to be made by the majority because there is some need to think about how minorities should react and it should be a dialogical negotiation'. Similarly, the historian, Humayun Ansari felt that Muslims in Britain could not make progress 'on the basis of values, norms and practices that evolved in largely non-Western/colonial contexts. It can only happen through the development of a synthesis commensurate with the Western environment'.

Ziauddin Sardar, while acknowledging that Britain was far more hospitable to difference than France or Germany, argued for the development of a 'European notion of multiculturalism' that would reflect the different histories and relationships between its constituent selves and also its particular relationship to Islam. He saw two main obstacles to the development of a 'true multiculturalism'. Firstly, the hegemonic nature of Western discourses that prioritise liberal individualism and thus cannot be reconciled with the ideal of 'multiculturalism'. The second is its failure to act as a transformative tool by which to challenge Western liberal values to allow for more 'inclusive forms':

> ... I would argue that we need a new notion of multiculturalism that is basically transformative and the transformation we are looking for is essentially transformation within the minority communities themselves so they have power and the space to be different. And then more important, transformation in the major community as well. The majority community has to in some cases, accept that some of its privileges are not deserved and so they have to hand those privileges in. Also in terms of power, so it's transformative in both cases, and it's not simply in terms of political power, it's in terms of intellectual power – in terms of how Britain or Europe sees Islam. So we're seeking transformation. Multiculturalism actually means that Europe has to learn to see Islam as a human culture, not as a demonised 'Other'...

Evaluation of Contemporary Britain as Multicultural

Throughout the interviews, 'multiculturalism' and its definitions were a recurring theme. Most participants remained cautious of the ways 'multiculturalism' as an ideology was used as an all encompassing framework to engage with racial difference yet was ambivalent regarding faith-based needs. The thinness of some multicultural approaches which focussed on superficial differences – the 'saris, steel bands and samosas' syndrome – and not enough on faith, spirituality and power relations, was a feature that many in our interviews had, through their respective roles, have been attempting to challenge and de-construct. While views were mixed, in the main respondents felt that multiculturalism in practice did not go far enough and was not adequately meeting the needs of Britain's faith communities. Many gave detailed responses either rooted in practice or theory, to the particular ways in which they felt multiculturalism as a project had or was, failing Muslim communities, especially Muslim women. These views can be contrasted with those cited earlier, which argued that multiculturalism had given way to those holding 'fundamentalist' religious views (Yuval-Davis, 1992).

British Multiculturalism as Superficial or Partial

Humera Khan, social activist and co-founder of the An-Nisa Society was one of the most critical of current multiculturalist policies in practice. For her, the superficiality of multiculturalism in practice was evident by the fact that most of the discussions simply consisted of continual battles against mis-representations, prejudice and a general unwillingness on the part of secularised institutions to negotiate with religion. Moreover, there was a tendency to view the multicultural as the 'fashionable' and superficial. This, she argued, left room for only a partial acceptance of difference which in turn manifests itself as rejection of the more significant and perhaps challenging facets to Muslim identities, describing this as a 'throw-back to colonialism':

> The way that it's developed really has been that you accept us for our food, you accept us for certain aspects of the way we dress, it's become a little bit fashionable, but you don't take the whole caboodle. I think this is where ordinary Muslims on the ground get really angry – that you don't want all of us; you just want a bit of us. In a sense, that is a sort of throwback to colonialism, where the European colonials came and just took what they wanted and didn't want to see the whole picture...

She recounted an experience at a sex education conference where in expressing a 'pro-chastity and pro-family' position, which seemed natural to Muslims and flowed from Islam, she says she was left 'feeling like a leper'.

British Multiculturalism as Excluding of Faith and Faith Identities

The most common criticism our respondents made of British multiculturalism was that it excludes faith and faith identities. Khan, taking further the point just noted above, articulated the centrality many Muslims attached to their faith and the failure of secularist, local and central government structures and bodies, in appreciating or accommodating this. Instead, she believed that Muslims were sometimes pressured into compromising on their religious identities in order to be accepted as part of the mainstream. This could be more explicitly explained through examples of social welfare practices which privileged ethnic and racial identities yet ignored faith-based identifications and needs. Its impact on Muslim women and families, for example, resulted in per-spectives and practices which problematised their needs and situated them within colonialist discourses of the 'helpless victim' in need of 'saving from cultural and religious oppression'.

Another example of the marginality of religion is anti-discrimination legislation, with religious discrimination in employment having been made unlawful only with effect from December 2003, almost four decades after the first racial discrimination legislation, a point made by Sacranie. He went on to emphasise not just the importance of religious identity but religious needs:

> ... I think the notion of multiculturalism must reflect the society we live in. And religion, faith plays a very important part, therefore that area has to be developed. Not just developed in terms of our identification in terms of identity, but in terms of our needs. In terms of how our argument comes out and that needs to be incorporated.

The absence of a strong faith element in society and its cost to Muslims through civil society as well as policy processes was highlighted by Ahmed Versi, Editor of *The Muslim News*, in relation to popular culture and the media. He felt that 'Hindu Indian culture' had successfully monopolised and influenced common understandings of the term 'Asian' in Britain. This he believed was expressed through the main-stream media which he felt tended to represent and encompass more Indian, 'Bollywood' manifestations of culture than faith perspectives, and in particular, at the expense of Muslim cultures. He linked this in with issues of resource allocation for community based projects, espe-cially with respect to the media, where description of a project as 'Asian' rather than by a religion was more likely to elicit a positive interest and yet it would probably, in his view, also promote 'Hindu' values:

> The classical example of multiculturalism – because it goes to race issues – when they talk about culture, they would say, 'Asian' or 'African' culture. I

mean 'Asian culture' is mainly Bollywood culture, and therefore you have the 'Meera Syal' kind of people coming through. It's got nothing to [do with] Muslims in a sense – there are Muslims who watch Bollywood, but we are talking about other issues, so if you look at any Asian programmes [in the name of] multiculturalism ... BBC Asian Network... there's hardly anything about the Muslim community as such.... Multiculturalism should include culture and practice of other faith communities, but Asian culture means Indian culture, nothing to do Muslim culture... These kinds of labels are used by many in the Indian community for resource allocations and to get up the ladder in TV...

Multiculturalism as a Two-way process

Based on the understanding that multiculturalism was a two-way process or dialogue, several respondents emphasised that in practice there is a lack of interaction. This was not only due to a failure of social structures to accommodate diverse needs, but also according to some, such as Maleiha Malik, partly due to Muslims themselves not engaging sufficiently with social structures, political processes or cultural dialogue at various levels. She went on to note, however, how debates on multiculturalism either failed to happen, or were distracted by more sensationalised comments such as from a Home Secretary on 'arranged marriages', for example. Similarly, Siddiqui argued that even amongst Muslims themselves there was a lack of intellectual space available for progressive discussions, and so 'dialogues had become monologues' where 'a lot of issues are clouded with theology, various cultural obsessions, religious obsessions'. These, he argued prevented the Muslim community from engaging not only with itself, but with social problems in any coherent, practical way and he regretted that Muslims did not reach out enough or have enough people with sufficient understanding to engage in cultural dialogue at all levels.

Power Imbalances

The issue of power was thought by many to be integral to the goals of multiculturalism. Power imbalances existed in key arenas of British society, where often subtle forms of power were at work. These were evident where minorities, especially Muslims, were absent or under-represented but could also be operative even where minority 'success' seemed apparent. Sardar, for example, reflected on this in relation to the media and the arts, where authors like Salman Rushdie, Hanif Koreshi, and Zadie Smith had won the most prestigious prizes but only certain representations were 'rewarded' or acknowledged whilst others were not:

> ... the deeper worry for me, is that success comes to those who play the role of the *'ethnic minorities' as appreciated and perceived by the dominant majority*. So these are the guys who are if you like, are contemporary 'Uncle Toms' or 'Brown Sahibs'. These are the guys who are playing to the gallery and they do 'ethnic stuff'. Now I'm a Muslim writer but I don't want to write about Islam all the time – I'm a British citizen, I regard myself as an intellectual so any newspaper can come and ask me what I think of the Iraq war, or what I think of the GM food crisis. So I want to be approached on my own, and not as a kind of dog who is going to perform tricks – and dogs who perform tricks are always rewarded.

More conventional power imbalances and lack of representation in the key social structures of British society were raised by several contributors. For instance, Shahid Malik talked of a 'deficit of power' in mainstream government positions and in political processes which contributed to a lack of adequate representation of Muslim needs at all levels. Yet, he, together with other political figures in the sample, such as Iqbal Sacranie and Farzana Hakim, Chief Advisor to the Chair (Trevor Philips) at the Commission for Racial Equality (CRE) and former 'Race' Advisor at No.10 Downing Street, noted how changes were taking place and Muslims had more access to the corridors of power since the arrival of New Labour in May 1997. Indeed, more than one of them thought that this change was more reflective of Tony Blair than of the government or political institutions as such; as Farzana Hakim notes:

> I find it quite weird though that the CRE hasn't moved (on faith); the Home Office has only just started to move and Downing Street did move a while ago but it didn't happen because of the machinery, it happened because of the individual ... No, I don't think Britain has coped with it [faith-based needs] at all; I think it's 'how do we deal with it?' and I think British people find it quite frightening actually...

Others were less pessimistic about what was happening and what was possible. Arguing that in comparison to other European countries such as Germany or France, British concepts of citizenship were accommodating and open to negotiation, Maleiha Malik took the view:

British Muslims are, in some respects, quite fortunate to live during a period in which there is I think a general effort to try and accommodate minorities. Not just British Muslims but all minority groups, but especially religious minorities, can use this to their advantage.

Accommodation of Religion in Public Life

Most of our interviewees remained positive about the possibilities for greater accommodation of faith-based needs within existing social structures and many also felt that religion – and the recognition of other faiths – could play a greater role in public institutions. The current relationship between Christianity as the traditionally dominant faith in Britain and the increasing secularism of social and political institutions still allowed for certain degrees of accommodation and recognition of faith within political structures. As Sacranie said:

> It's a society that is very strongly influenced by people with secular views. Christianity is the dominant religion; the Anglican church is the established church but it doesn't mean that everything revolves around them. They have recognised that other faith communities and other sections of non-faith communities can play an equal part. So what we are saying is that the time will come when Islam, and other faith communities will have the same opportunities.

None in our sample viewed secularism as a homogeneous concept and whilst there was a certain degree of criticism reserved for those believed to hold 'extremist secular' perspectives, there was a general sense that 'liberal secularism' could, in theory, accommodate diverse cultural and religious needs. Whilst none advocated the introduction of Muslim Personal Laws into Britain as a separate framework, for example, the majority of our contributors wanted to see religion play a greater role in public life and expressed confidence that Church-influenced structures, as a result of expanding interfaith dialogues, provided appropriate avenues forward.

However, a significant minority of our respondents felt the need to state that there were proper limits upon religion in public life. For example, Sarfraz Manzoor (journalist and broadcaster), said that 'one's religion should not interfere into one's workplace'. Ansari noted that 'in practice, the ideology of secularism seems to be intolerant of other world views and operates in illiberal ways' but still felt that secularism held out the best promise for tolerance:

... I feel that institutional life needs to be less influenced by any religion. For instance, I feel that discussion of all religions in schools should take place on the basis of equality and in critically balanced (various 'insider' and 'outsider' perspectives woven in) way. I would argue for the dis-establishment of the Church of England and the abolition of the existing blasphemy law. ... Politically, I would be closer to the 'secularist' as opposed to the 'Islamist' perspective.

For Maleiha Malik, for whom liberal political theory and western legal models were as important a normative guide as her readings in and understanding of Islam, what was critical was to achieve a just and viable balance:

The challenge is to try to negotiate some sort of settlement which strikes the right balance between acceptance in the public sphere but also a recognition that their values, or their religion, can't provide the basis for all decision-making in the public sphere. Multiculturalism as part of a strategy to accommodate the most important aspects of the identity of citizens as far as possible is important to them, is a good idea. What's important now in terms of how that's going to be given shape is to try and give that central idea some sort of more concrete, legal and political foundation. There are good examples of countries where that's been done quite well. Canada is quite a good example of a country where multiculturalism is taken quite seriously.

Conclusion

It is clear that though 'moderate' or mainstream Muslims represent a variety of views, they are pro-multiculturalism as long as it includes faith as a positive dimension of 'difference'. They are very conscious that British advocates of multiculturalism have only belatedly, tentatively and slowly come to extend and deepen the ideas of multiculturalism to include faith communities. The concern that Muslims are uncomfortable with pluralism may be misplaced (Parekh, 2003). Indeed, some of this group of Muslims believe that the Qur'an, Islam and Muslim history are powerful sources of multiculturalism and religious pluralism and represent a superior form of multiculturalism than has been developed elsewhere or is on offer in the contemporary West.

This ideal of Islamic multiculturalism is faith-based in identifying dimensions of 'difference', with other religions not just included but given primacy in terms of respect. It probably also is faith-based in terms of limits of recognition, with critically, homosexuality, more likely to be positioned as what is tolerated rather than respected. The plurality within this ideal is mainly communal. If Muslim societies have had difficulties in ensuring the protection of individuals within communities, this was not an issue that our respondents raised. Finally, it was recognised that Muslim pluralism has historically existed where there has been one dominant or over-arching faith, where Muslims were able to put their ideal into practice. There was no discussion of historical cases of successful pluralism where Muslims were a minority. On the other hand, there were few positive references to pluralism in contemporary Muslim societies and which might be exemplars, with the exception of a singular but fulsome reference to Malaysia.

Most of the other aspects of the multicultural ideal and criticisms of contemporary British practice, such as the distinction between mutual respect and tolerance, the importance of non-separateness and dialogue, the need for transformative change on the part of the minorities as well as the majority seem to us to be very similar to the views held by non-Muslim British multiculturalists (Parekh, 2000 and CMEB, 2000; though *cf* Sardar, 2002 and 2004). Some of the respondents explicitly drew on western multicultural theory and practice in order to pose limits to ideas that others derived from Islam, such as those to do with sexuality and the secular.

So both Islam and Muslim history, on the one hand, and contemporary western multicultural theory and practice, on the other hand, were drawn upon though in differing degrees and suggesting different syntheses. The important point to conclude is not that all non-militant Muslims agree on these matters, nor that there is no tension between Muslim and western ideals. Rather, it is clear that there is much overlap between the two, with some creative tension and enough scope for dialogue and negotiation, contrary to the 'clash of civilisations' thesis.

It will also have been evident that the category of Muslim intellectual/ activist – the kind of person who speaks in and for the Muslim public sphere in Britain – includes some whose 'authority' to speak does not primarily lie in expertise with scriptural texts and traditional Islamic scholarship. While many of the reformist and radical Muslims of the nineteenth and twentieth centuries have been lay intellectuals (Hassan

Al Banna, Syed Qutb, Abul Ala Maududi, Rashid Ghannoushi to name a few) and have been enormously and globally influential, the individuals our project has studied are primarily experts in using and engaging with contemporary western discourses; in this and perhaps also in their commitment to identifying and serving the interests of British Muslims, they may, therefore, be a new kind of Muslim public figure.

APPENDIX
'Moderate' Muslims – Interview list

1. Lord Nazir Ahmed — Labour Party Member of the House of Lords. The first Muslim peer.

2. Navid Akhtar — Documentary film-maker and journalist.

3. Anas Altikriti — Media spokesperson for the Muslim Association of Britain. Came to prominence in the anti-war movements following September 11.

4. Humayun Ansari OBE — Professor of History of Islam and Cultural Diversity. Director, Centre for Ethnic Minority Studies, Royal Holloway, University of London

5. Farzana Hakim — Principal Advisor to the Chair, Commission for Racial Equality; former advisor on race relations to the Prime Minister.

6. Humera Khan — Co-Founder of the Muslim women's group, the An-Nisa Society, London.

7. Yusuf Al-Khoei — Director of the Al-Khoei Foundation, London. Trustee of Forum Against Islamophobia and Racism..

8. Maleiha Malik — Professor in Law, King's College, London University

9. Shahid Malik — Former MP for Dewsbury, Member of the Labour Party National Executive Council and former Commissioner at the Commission for Racial Equality.

10. Sarfraz Mansoor — Journalist and Broadcaster

11. Fuad Nahdi — Editor-in-Chief, *Q-News*, The Muslim Magazine

12. Aki Nawaz — Head of *Nation Records* and lead of political band Fun-Da-Mental.

13. Tariq Ramadan	Professor at St. Antony's College, University of Oxford, and probably the best known Muslim intellectual in Western Europe.
14. Sir Iqbal Sacranie	Secretary General, Muslim Council of Britain.
15. Ziauddin Sardar	Writer, Broadcaster, cultural critic and Commissioner, Commission for Equality and Human Rights
16. Bobby Sayyid	Research Fellow, University of Leeds.
17. Massoud Shadjareh	Chairman of the Islamic Human Rights Commission, London.
18. Ghayasuddin Siddiqui	Head of the community-based forum, the Muslim Parliament and Director of an Islamic think-tank, The Muslim Institute.
19. Ahmed Versi	Editor of the monthly, *The Muslim News*.
20. Abdel Wahhab El-Affendi	Senior Research Fellow at the Centre for the Study of Democracy, University of Westminster.
21. Merryl Wyn Davies	Writer and Broadcaster.

Informal conversations were also had with Sheikhs the late Dr Zaki Badawi and Hamza Yusuf.

Notes

1 From: *Theory, Culture and Society*, Special Issue on Authority and Islam, 24 (2), March 2007, co-authored with Fauzia Ahmad; being an expanded version of a paper presented at 'Global Islam And Democracy Conference', January 2004, University of Bristol. We are grateful to SAGE Publications for permission to republish and to the Calouste Gulbenkian Foundation for a small grant to fund the research.

2 The 'hijacking' theme was in fact most notably introduced by a charismatic, white US convert to Islam, Sheikh Hamza Yusuf who was consulted by President Bush immediately after 9/11 but soon fell out of favour with the White House. His views were promoted by the magazine of the young Muslim professionals in Britain, *Q News* (eg in the November 2001 issue). Dr Muqtedar Khan, Director of International Studies, Adrian College, Michigan had an even more uncompromisingly 'moderate' statement in the right-wing, tabloid newspaper, *The Sun*, but was not taken up by British Muslims, or the British media with comparable levels of enthusiasm (see Khan 2002).

3 It should also be noted that a large proportion of Muslims representing varied political and religious sympathies can also object to the term 'British Muslim' preferring instead to talk of themselves as 'a Muslim in Britain'. Indeed there were a minority within our sample who expressed such sentiments but this did not contradict their sense of

being part of Britain. Bobby Sayyid for example, rejected the term 'British Muslim' as he believed that Muslim subjectivities transcend 'all other political identities'. It also represented the sub-ordination of an Islamic identity to a nationalist one:

> ...where Islam is still considered to be exterior to Britain – its not part of that narrative and if you really believe in Islam then you also have to accept that Islam does not belong to any space or any time and that its for everyone and we're for everything. Therefore, what is the point of calling yourself a British Muslim? To differentiate yourself from who? From other Muslims and why?

Attempts to 'nationalise or vernacularise Islam' were therefore potentially dangerous to its continued existence.

4 When showing a final draft of this paper to our interviewees, a few commented on how 7/7 had forced some British Muslim organisations to acknowledge the attraction some extremist movements held amongst some young British Muslims, but also the need for more concerted efforts to educate against extremism. For instance, Yousif al-Khoei, Director of the Al-Khoei Foundation, London said:

> My own view is that due to a combination of factors – mainstream Muslim organisations and institutions have not been able to counter the disproportionate weight and louder voice of the few extremists who have hijacked the good name of Islam. 7/7 was a turning point in galvanising the voice of the silent majority who began to see the enormity of the damage caused and reclaim the rich legacy of reason, peace and co existence within Islam.

This sentiment was also reflected in several newspaper and magazine articles by prominent Muslims.

5 Of course 'Muslim community' is no more a singular, undifferentiated term than, say, 'woman' or 'working class' or 'British' but if this was to inhibit the use of such internally differentiated and complex concepts, or even to inhibit marking them by a singular noun, speech, let alone social science, would be impossible (Modood, 1994 and 2007).

6 Many Muslims, within a British context at least, distinguish between 'fanatics' and 'fundamentalists', in order to re(appropriate) the latter term (as black people in the US and UK have earlier done with 'black', turning a derogatory term into a proud identity). 'Fanatic' represents a follower of a rigid and authoritarian version of Islam. It is sought, however, to give 'fundamentalist' a positive meaning: someone who adheres to the fundamentals of their faith; an aspiration of all of the devout. Attempts to challenge negative connotations of 'fundamentalist' can take unusual forms; for example, through the naming of the popular music group 'Fun-da-mental', led by Aki Nawaz, one of our interviewees.

7 Worthy of some mention here is one of the more recent and controversial developments within the 'Progressive Muslim' movement in the US. In a single act of defiance against commonly held religious doctrine, one the Progressive movements leading female scholars, Professor Amina Wadud, led a mixed group of men and women in Friday prayers in March 2005. Her actions naturally sparked a heated debate amongst Muslims, not only for her actions but her rationale; she is alleged to have challenged the authority of the Qur'an by stating that she 'did not agree with the Qur'an' (Baksh, 2005).

8 There may be a group of people who may possibly fit all the above criteria but who it would not be correct to interpret as 'moderate Muslims'. They are persons who may be from a Muslim background but who are publicly hostile to public Islam and to Muslim community politics (eg Salman Rushdie, Hanif Kureshi, Tariq Ali).

9 Similar meanings of 'moderate' are identified as the dominant meanings among Muslims by the American academic, Muqtedar Khan but he wants to save the term and defines a 'moderate' Muslim as a Muslim whose quest for social justice is through the spirit of *ijtihad*, www.ijitihad.org/moderatemuslims.htm For an overview of American Muslim political discourses, see Leonard 2003; for a European Muslim intervention, see Ramadan 2004a.

10 Tim Winter, a white English convert to Islam and academic (whose Muslim name is Abdul Hakim Murad), divides Muslims into the 'mainstream', who seek spiritual nourishment and peace of mind, and a small minority of 'zealots' and 'liberals', both of whom are overly influenced by western thought and secularism (Winter, 2003). This is a perspective also shared by the prominent and popular regular visitor from the US, Shaikh Hamza Yusuf Hanson, who we spoke to informally. A group of, mainly American, Muslims have come together under the label 'Progressive Muslims' to interpret Islam for the twenty-first century focused on social justice, gender and pluralism and with equal respect for all communities (Safi, 2003:3).

11 Shadid and Van Koningsveld (1996) themselves want to argue that some European Muslims realise the 'Territory of Islam' and 'Territory of War' dichotomy is unhelpful and are developing a third category, 'Territory of Covenant'. Our point is that none of our respondents referred to the dichotomy and so analysing British Muslim thinking today in terms of a critical engagement with this dichotomy is an inadequate way of framing the issues we are concerned with.

12 This was the emphatic view of one of the TCS anonymous reviewers of this article.

13 A more widely organised focus of opposition to al-Qaradawi's visit was based on his endorsement of violent resistance to Israeli occupation of Palestine, illustrating how this issue too is central to the political accommodation of Muslims in Britain and elsewhere but clashes with the views and power of supporters of Israel. In order to contain this clash and develop positive links, there are now some Jewish-Muslim dialogue groups such as Calamus-Maimonides, Alif-Aleph and Discursis. However, the issue remains sensitive on both sides and it has been argued that the critique of Zionism is 'one area in which most Muslims in Britain have a similar position' (Sayyid, 2003).

14 It is sadly ironic that such an integrationist is reviled by many French intellectuals and has been denied entry into the US (Ramadan, 2004b), and was the target of a boycott attempt by the National Union of Students, who tried to exclude him from the 2004 European Social Forum (www2.mpacuk.org).

8

Multiculturalism after 7/7:
A Scapegoat or A Hope For the Future?

From the *RUSI Journal*, April 2008[1]

'Risk, Threat and Security, the case of the United Kingdom' (Prins and Salisbury, 2008) expresses the consensus of a recent high ranking security seminar. Amongst the various views expressed is the claim of a misplaced deference to multiculturalism, which failed to lay down the line to immigrants, has contributed to a lack of national self-confidence and a fragmenting society that has been exploited by Islamist terrorists (pp22-23). That most of the individuals involved in the London bombings of 7/7 and some other bombing plots were born and/or brought up in Britain, a country that had given them or their parents a refuge from persecution, fear or poverty, and freedom of worship, seems to have led many to conclude that multiculturalism has failed – or, worse still, to blame it for the bombings. For example, Gilles Keppel observed that the bombers 'were the children of Britain's own multicultural society' and the bombings have smashed multicultura-lism to smithereens (Keppel, 2005:2). William Pfaff stated the view, 'these British bombers are a consequence of a misguided and catas-trophic pursuit of multiculturalism' (Pfaff, 2005), and Martin Wolf con-cluded that 'multiculturalism must be discarded as nonsense' (Wolf, 2005).

Of course multiculturalism has many critics today and not all of them believe that it is responsible for the bombings that are a threat to British

security; many simply believe that it has failed to emphasise commonalities and not achieved integration. This criticism predates 7/7 or even
9/11. For example, the shift at the Home Office from Jack Straw's multiculturalism to David Blunkett's community cohesionism was the result
of their own politics and as a response to the disturbances in some of
the Northern cities in the early summer of 2001. Yet it is the more radical
thesis that Prins and Salisbury argue.

Consensus without Evidence

I find their thesis implausible, at the very least exaggerated. Firstly, it
suffers from a lack of evidence. No key theorist or text of multiculturalism is cited. Admittedly, this is not usually possible in short magazine
or newspaper articles but it is astonishing how the general thesis that
'multiculturalism is dead and was killed by 9/11 and/or 7/7' has become part of the (inter)national common sense without any reference
to the work of any key multiculturalist theorist or text. I think most
informed people would accept that the key international theorists of
multiculturalism (throwing the net as wide as we can) include figures
such as Charles Taylor, Iris Marion Young, Stuart Hall, Bhikhu Parekh,
Will Kymlicka and Paul Gilroy. Yet none of these authors, indeed any
multiculturalists at all, are cited in the various fora speeches, print, tele-
vision, radio and web items in which the national common sense is
repeated again and again. Instead, the critics all simply cite each other.
I have now been party to a number of public debates on this topic and
when I have challenged speakers for evidence of this view about multiculturalism, the response is usually of the kind that I am just being
pedantic as everyone knows that the truth of the view has been proven.
Yet no multiculturalist literature is cited and no evidence is offered linking multiculturalism to terrorism. A particularly regrettable case is that
of the Chief Rabbi Jonathan Sacks' new book, *The Home We Build
Together* (2007). Central to the argument of the book is a critique of
multiculturalism; moreover, at the end of the book is a bibliography
with a section entitled 'On Multiculturalism' containing some of the
works of the theorists I have mentioned above. Yet none of these works
are referred to, let alone analysed, in Sacks' critique.

It may be that the non-academic critics of multiculturalists are not
interested in engaging with academic texts and perhaps are not even

blaming those texts for the outcomes they attribute to multiculturalism. Perhaps they have in mind the practitioners of multiculturalism, the doers, the policy makers and implementers, the politicians, bureaucrats and public professionals, or indeed just a certain 'climate of opinion'. If so, again no evidence of any kind is offered showing a linkage between the promotion of multiculturalism and the deleterious effects on national confidence, let alone security. In fact, as far as I know, no such social science evidence exists at the moment.

What is Multiculturalism?

A second and more fundamental problem flows from the first. Because no reference is made to the international literature of multiculturalism, the critics define multiculturalism not by referring to what advocates of multiculturalism think it is but by what other critics think it is. So I would like to remedy this. I would like to show that multiculturalism is not about separatism, fragmentation or tolerating the growth of terrorist networks. I offer a view that is my own, based as it is on my book, *Multiculturalism: A Civic Idea* (2007) but it is recognisably a view of multiculturalism as found in the political theory and related literature.

The ideal of multicultural citizenship is a critique of the cultural assimilation traditionally demanded by nation-states of migrants and minorities, as well as of that liberal individualism that has no space for groups. Nevertheless, it is clearly grounded in and is a development out of the ideas of individual equality and democratic citizenship. It is not about pre-democratic arrangements such as the Ottoman accommodation of minorities through the *millet* system. It seeks to pluralise, and hence adapt not undermine, the unity and equality of citizenship and national identity.

For multicultural citizenship is based on the idea that citizens have individual rights but citizens are not uniform and their citizenship contours itself around them. In other words, citizenship is not a monistic identity that is completely apart from or transcends other identities important to citizens. These group identities are ever present and each group has a right to be a part of the civic whole and to speak up for itself and for its vision of the whole.

The concepts of equality and of citizenship that are being appealed to can be sketched further by reference to Charles Taylor's suggestion that when we talk about equality in the context of race, sex, ethnicity and so on, we are appealing to two different albeit related concepts – *equal dignity*, and *equal respect* (Taylor, 1994). Equal dignity appeals to people's humanity or to some specific membership like citizenship and applies to all members in a relatively uniform way. We appeal to this idea in relation to anti-discrimination policies where we appeal to the principle that everybody should be treated the same. But Taylor, and other theorists in differing ways (*cf* Parekh, 2000), also posit the idea of *equal respect*. If equal dignity focuses on what people have in common and so is gender-blind, colour-blind and so on, equal respect is based on an understanding that difference is also important in conceptualising and institutionalising equal relations between individuals.

This is because individuals have group identities and these may be the ground of existing and long-standing inequalities such as racism, for example, and the ways that some people have conceived and treated others as inferior, less rational and culturally backward. While those conceptions persist they will affect the dignity of non-white people, above all where they share a social life with white people which is steeped in negative images of non-white peoples. The negative conceptions will lead to direct and indirect acts of discrimination – they will eat away at the possibilities of equal dignity. They will affect the self-understanding of those who breathe in and seek to be equal participants in a culture in which ideas of their inferiority, or even just of their absence, their invisibility, is pervasive. They will stand in need of self-respect and the respect of others, of the dominant group; the latter will be crucial, for it is the source of their damaged self-respect and it is where the power for change lies. The imperative for equal respect, the turning of negative group identities into positive ones, then, flows out of a commitment to equal dignity.

There is, then, deep resonance between citizenship and multicultural recognition. Not only do both presuppose complementary notions of unity and plurality, and of equality and difference, but the idea of respect for the group self-identities that citizens value is central to citizenship. Moreover, seeing citizenship as a work in progress and as partly constituted, and certainly extended, by critical ongoing dialogues and

novel demands for due recognition, as circumstances shift, means that citizenship can be understood as conversations and re-negotiations, not just about who is to be recognised but about what is recognition, about the terms of citizenship itself. At one point, it is the injuries of class that demand civic attention; at another there is a plea for dropping a self-deluding 'colour-blindness' and of addressing racialised statuses through citizenship. The one thing that civic inclusion does not consist of is an uncritical acceptance of an existing conception of citizenship, of 'the rules of the game" and a one-sided 'fitting-in' of new entrants or the new equals (the ex-subordinates). To be a citizen, no less than to have
-just become a citizen, is to have a right to not just be recognised but to debate the terms of recognition.

Re-emphasising the Civic and the National

Even though new interpretations of civic integration is the hallmark of the political theory of multiculturalism, I am willing to concede to critics of multiculturalism that sometimes this aspect becomes muted. We in Europe unfortunately do sometimes think that the national and the multicultural are incompatible. In other parts of the world where multiculturalism has been adopted as a state project or as a national project – in Canada, Australia and Malayasia for example — it has not just been coincidental with, but integral to, a nation-building project: to creating Canadians, Aussies and Malayasians. Even in the US, where the federal state has had a much lesser role in the multicultural project, the incorporation of ethno-religious diversity and hyphenated Americans (such as Italian-Americans) has been about country-making, civic inclusion and making a claim upon the national identity. It is Europeans who are likely to think of multiculturalism as antithetical to, rather than as a reformer of, national citizenship.

Even so, such a view has been much more characteristic of say Germany or France than Britain. In Britain, some anti-racists of the 1970s and 1980s thought of, say, black identity and Britishness as historically deeply oppositional. But since that time race and multiculturalism has steadily arisen as a national issue and has increasingly been viewed in integrationist terms. Yet it has had two features (in each case the contrast with France and Germany is notable) that unsettle some people and which do not fit more traditional or deferential notions of integration or assimilation (when most European politicians say 'integration' they usually mean 'assimilation'). Firstly, the political salience of the issue has been accompanied, perhaps even driven by the active and voluble participation, even the leadership of some of the ethnic minorities. In France and Germany the political debates have been *about*, not *with* the migrants and their offspring. In Britain members of the ethnic minorities have not only pushed for these debates and participated in them but they have contributed to setting the terms of the debates. Secondly, this has come to mean that these debates involve rethinking 'integration' and 'Britain' – which is another way of saying that these debates have had a multiculturalist character.

This has made Britain a pioneer of this politics in Europe but it has sometimes led to one-sided emphases. Critically, it does not make sense to encourage strong multicultural or minority identities and weak common or national identities; strong multicultural identities are a good thing – they are not intrinsically divisive, reactionary or fifth columns – but they need a framework of vibrant, dynamic national narratives and the ceremonies and rituals which give expression to a national identity. It is clear that minority identities are capable of having an emotional pull for the individuals for whom they are important. Multicultural citizenship requires, therefore, if it is to be equally attractive to the same individuals, a comparable counter-balancing emotional pull. National identity can play this role. Many Britons, for example, say they are worried about disaffection amongst some Muslim young men and more generally a lack of identification with Britain amongst many Muslims in Britain (Uberoi and Modood, 2010). As a matter of fact, surveys over many years have shown Muslims have been reaching out for an identification with Britain. For example, in a Channel 4 NOP survey done in Spring 2006, 82 per cent of a national sample of Muslims said they felt very strongly (45%) or fairly strongly (37%) that they belonged to Britain. Yet the survey also found that many Muslims did not feel comfortable in Britain. For example, 58 per cent thought that extreme religious persecution of Muslims was very likely (23%) or fairly likely (35%)[2]. Similarly, a recent Gallup Poll of Londoners found that 57 per cent of Muslims identified strongly with Britain compared to 48 per cent of non-Muslims, yet 54 per cent of the capital's Muslims think more should be done to accommodate their religion (Mogahed and Nyiri, 2007).

It is therefore to be welcomed that Gordon Brown, as Prime Minister, argued for the need to revive and revalue British national identity. He seeks to derive a set of core values (liberty, fairness, enterprise and so on) from a historical narrative. Yet such values, even if they could singly or in combination be given a distinctive British take, are too complex and their interpretation and priority too contested to be set into a series of meaningful definitions. Every public culture must operate through shared values, which are both embodied in and used to criticise its institutions and practices, but they are not simple and uniform and their meaning is discursively grasped as old interpretations are dropped and new circumstances unsettle one consensus and another is built up. Simply saying that freedom or equality is a core British value is unlikely to settle any controversy or tell us, for example, what is hate speech and how it should be handled. Definitions of core values will either be too bland or too divisive.

More fundamentally, the idea that there has to be a schedule of 'non-negotiable' value statements to which every citizen is expected to sign up is not in the spirit of a open, plural, dialogical citizenship. The national identity should be woven in debate and discussion, not re-duced to a list. Central to it is a citizenship and the right of all, especially previously marginalised or newly admitted groups to make a claim on the national identity. In this way, racism and other forms of stigmatised identities can be challenged and supplanted by a positive politics of mutual respect and inclusion. Being black or Muslim is then no longer seen as something to be tolerated but part of what it is to be British today.

Seen in this way, we should – to return to where I started – distinguish between those who want to rightly emphasise a civic re-balancing of what some have seen as a one-sided multiculturalism, from those who think that multiculturalism is out of date (Meer and Modood, 2009).

In doing so, we make clear that multiculturalism is not about separate communities, peaceful co-existence or mere toleration. It is about civic engagement which unpicks the negative treatment of 'difference' – stereotypes, racism, Islamophobia and so on – and the reform of institutions and public culture so minority identities are not ignored or confined to a private sphere but woven into a multicultural Britishness.

Multiculturalism, then, is not just about minority identities but all of us opening up our sense of 'We' and making space for others and so creating a new, plural 'We'. That is the integration that should be our local and national goal.

Not only has multiculturalism nothing to do with the conditions that breed alienation, social divisions, national decline and terrorism; it is a project to avoid these outcomes. This is not just about the defence of a political idea. The simplistic linkage between home-grown terrorism and the multicultural project is unfair because it ends up blaming not just national policies but specific communities for particular outcomes. In this case, Muslims as a whole are blamed for terrorism, for not standing up to extremism and for not integrating. This is not only unfair but also divisive, and so not likely to achieve the much-sought for integration. Indeed, this is the pertinence of multiculturalism: it seeks integration without stigmatising groups or threatening their identities. And looking beyond domestic issues to the wider geo-political setting, pitting British national interest against political Islam is not a wise policy if national unity is a priority. So, given recent foreign policy, it would be foolish to be too optimistic about the success of any domestic policies of multiculturalism. The point is that the latter are nevertheless not the source of some of the divisions in our society today, but a source of hope.

Notes

1 From: *The RUSI Journal*, The Royal United Services Institute, vol. 153 (2), April, 2008, pp. 14-17

2 See <http://www.channel4.com/news/microsites/D/dispatches2006/muslim_survey/index.html>

9

The Rise of St George

From *Western Daily Press*, April 2005

There is a rising call for the English to be more conscious of their national identity, with David Blunkett's speech being one of the most recent cases. It is certainly a much uncelebrated identity. Having spent St Patrick's Day in New York last week I know what it means to the Irish, wherever they may be, and having a Welsh wife, I know about the leek and the daffodil on St David's Day. In contrast, most people in England don't even know the date of St George's Day.

Yet, it has to be said that English nationalism can be an ugly fearful thing. One thinks of the yobbish football fans – thankfully less common today than a few years ago – that take their aggression to European cities, causing mayhem and bring shame and dishonour to the name of 'England'. For many people, that kind of racism and violence is what English nationalism is about and hence it's a blessing that English identity should not feature too large in the life of this country.

British blacks and Asians, the large majority of whom are in England, in particular know from first hand what flag-waving nationalism, with or without booze and football, can mean. They are as likely to be as nervous as anyone about 'celebrating' England. Not only are they likely to be excluded from the party but are likely to be blamed for whatever nationalists moan about, especially those who hark back to Empire and racial purity.

Nevertheless, I am on Blunkett's side on this one. I always found it odd, even shameful, that in the 1970s and 1980s the National Front and the BNP were allowed to wave the Union Jack without protest – in fact they were the only people to do so. We have now rightly reclaimed the Union Jack from the racists and have seen the pride with which heroes like Daley Thompson and Frank Bruno, and most recently Olympiads like Kelly Holmes and Amir Khan, have held it aloft with pride. It has rightly become a symbol of inclusivity and a multi-ethnic country.

Isn't it time to go the same way with St. George's flag? When Scottish football fans used to come down in their tens of thousands to Wembley in the 1990s waving the St. Andrews flag, the English were made to feel silly responding with the Union Jack and God Save the Queen – after all, those things are as much Scottish as they are English. The scorn of the Scots at the lack of English symbols stimulated the use of St George's flag and it has grown and grown as we saw at last summer's European Cup.

If it was most flown on white working class estates and by 'White Van Man', it has also been embraced by many young Asians and blacks. My generation of ethnic minorities have struggled to be included as British. We thought of 'English' as a kind of cultural and ethnic identity belonging to white people but were determined to stake our claim to be British.

Our next generation, however, does think of itself as English – sometimes more English than British – and does not think of English as being about white but as reflecting today's multi-ethnic cities, especially compared to the rest of Britain. For them Englishness is not racism by the backdoor.

It is essential that English celebrations should be inclusive and embrace multi-ethnicity and strengthen our sense of belonging to a common country, not create obstacles. Moreover, it should include civic values and be supportive of British political institutions – 'English' should not be an exclusionary or a separatist identity. Britain is a nest of identities and none should be too big for the nest, or, worse, threaten the nest itself.

By these criteria the new English identity is far too simplistic and far from ideal – it is too male, white, working class, right wing and centred on competitive sport. But this is not a reason to disparage it: it is for the rest of us to extend it and remake it so that it includes us too.

Ethnic minority people are making a major contribution to sport and feature most prominently in the England football team but we are also part of contemporary music, fashion, comedy, literature and the arts in England. These things are part of what it means to be English today, and are what people in other countries know and admire when they think of England.

Interestingly, tourists are attracted to these things when they visit England – not just Buckingham Palace and the Houses of Parliament. Our intellectuals, science and universities, the BBC and quality journalism are also more applauded abroad than here.

The same is true of the multicultural mixing of cities like London, which is the envy of many American and European cities. To be English is much more than to support a football team that last won something in 1966.

10

Is Multiculturalism Dead?

From *Public Policy Research*, June-August, 2008[1]

How is a balance to be struck between the need to treat people equally, the need to treat people differently, and the need to maintain shared values and social cohesion? (CMEB, 2000:40)

A certain kind of modest, communitarian, ethno-religious multi-culturalism, self-consciously incorporating and building on ideas of institutional racism and anti-discrimination, seemed to be rolling forward in the 1990s and the first few years of this century. It found expression in the Commission on Multi-Ethnic Britain (CMEB) report *The Future of Multi-Ethnic Britain* (the Parekh Report) (2000), as well as in some New Labour initiatives. The latter included the Lawrence Inquiry, the Race Relations Amendment Act (2000), the funding of Muslim schools, the multiplying of ethnic minority peers, religious discrimination legislation, and the introduction of the reli-gion question into the 2001 Census.

But from about the middle of 2001, with the disturbances in the northern towns and, later, the 9/11 attacks, the mood began to shift, and, within a few years, most public commentators pronounced multi-culturalism dead. I do not want to directly discuss this backlash. Nor can I here discuss recent public policy, though I believe an analysis would show that the Government has qualified, rather than aban-doned, multiculturalism (Meer and Modood, 2009). Rather, I would like to look at some of the criticisms of multiculturalism, which I think deserve to be considered seriously.

117

My view is that none of these criticisms mean the 'end of multi-culturalism', and each can and should be taken on board to some extent. I think, however, that these ideas can be grouped under those that are generally seen as qualifying multiculturalism, and those that are seen as fundamentally opposed to it.

Ideas Qualifying Multiculturalism

1. Basic Human Rights

I do not think that anyone seriously disputes that the kind of multi-culturalism appropriate to Britain must be in a context of human rights (the CMEB report had a chapter on human rights), but few are persuaded that multicultural equality (any more than other forms of social equality) can be derived from human rights.

2. Gender Equality

We have increasingly become aware that some forms of abuse of women are disproportionately found in some minority communities (for example, clitorodotomy, forced marriages). Unfortunately, feminism has come to be used as a missionary ideology to express the supremacy of the west and the backwardness of the rest. While this is mainly on the right, the tendency is not absent on the left. Moreover, in terms of practical politics, it is clear that some of these problems could be seriously tackled only through the cooperation of the relevant communities. Strident and authoritarian approaches are likely to be counter-productive, and create besieged, stigmatised communities.

For these kinds of reasons there has become a regrettable polarisation on these sorts of issues. But the common ground is actually considerable. For multiculturalists clearly do not support violence, coercion or the undermining of the legal equality of women, though there will also be a few limited areas where people will disagree about what constitutes equality. I do not have space here to discuss such cases but can support the main point I am making here by pointing to Anne Phillips' argument (Phillips, 2007) that gender equality and multiculturalism are not intrinsically opposed.

3. Ongoing Immigration, Superdiversity

We have recently experienced, are experiencing and, it is argued, will continue to experience, large-scale immigration. Given the diversity of the locations from whence migrants are coming, the result is not communities, but a churning mass of languages, ethnicities and religions, all cutting across each other and creating a 'superdiversity' (Vertovec, 2006). But it does not follow that the settled, especially postcolonial, communities, who have a particular historical relationship with Britain, lose their political significance.

4. Transnationalism

It is argued that globalisation, migration and telecommunications have created populations dispersed across countries that interact more with each other, and have a greater sense of loyalty to each other, than they might to their fellow citizens. Diasporic links like this certainly exist, and are likely to increase, but I am unconvinced that the net result is an inevitable erosion of national citizenship: British African-Caribbeans and South Asians have families in their countries of origin and in the US and Canada, but there is little evidence that most, or even any, branches of those families do not feel British, American, Canadian, etc.

Challenges to Multiculturalism

1. Community Cohesion/Citizenship/Common Values/Britishness

I group all these terms together, but I appreciate they do not all mean the same thing, and some will emphasise one more than the others, and might even deem one of the set unnecessary. Nevertheless, each of these concepts has recently been invoked as embodying the kind of commonality that members of British society need to have, and which is said to have been obscured by a fetish of difference.

It is argued that Britain as a society and a state has been too *laissez-faire* in promoting commonality and this must now be remedied. Hence, the introduction of measures such as swearing a US-style oath of allegiance at naturalisation ceremonies (as recommended by the CMEB), an English language proficiency requirement when seeking citizenship, and citizenship education for migrants and, indeed, in all secondary schools.

119

Many advocates of this approach also choose to say something positive about multiculturalism, and suggest that they are seeking to amend it by emphasising that what multiculturalism fails to appreciate is the necessary wider framework for its success. I would say this is true of Bernard Crick, Ted Cantle, and the Commission on Integration and Cohesion among others, including most government statements, at least during Blair.

On the other hand, others promote versions of this view by expressly framing it in terms of 'multiculturalism is dead'. While on the right, multiculturalism is seen as always having been mistaken (for example, columnist and author Melanie Phillips, 2006 and Conservative Shadow Education Secretary, Michael Gove, 2006), a more centrist, and some-times left, view is that multiculturalism was right for its time, but that time is over (for example, the Chair of the Equalities and Human Rights Commission, Trevor Phillips and the Editor of Prospect, David Good-hart). A major, recent example of this position is to be found in Chief Rabbi Sacks' 2007 book *The Home We Build Together* (Sacks, 2007), when, in his earlier books, he has been an eloquent exponent of com-munitarian pluralism.

Such critics substantiate their views by quoting each other, rather than analysing the texts of multiculturalists. This is not surprising, as the political theorists of multiculturalism see it as a project of inclusivity, and this was how the CMEB also saw it.

The best that can be said for this view is that, perhaps, we in Europe are more likely to think that the national and the multicultural are incom-patible. In other parts of the world, where multiculturalism has been adopted as a state project or as a national project – in Canada, Australia and Malaysia for example – it has not just been coincidental with, but at times integral to, a nation-building project.

Moreover, it does not make sense to encourage strong multicultural or minority identities and weak common or national identities. Strong multicultural identities are a good thing – they are not intrinsically divi-sive, reactionary or fifth columns – but they need a framework of vibrant, dynamic, national narratives, and the ceremonies and rituals that give expression to a national identity. The national identity should, however, be woven in debate and discussion, not reduced to a list of imposed values. For, central to it is citizenship, and the right of all, especially previously marginalised or newly admitted groups, to make a claim on the national identity. In this way, racism and other forms of stigmatised identities can be challenged and supplanted by a positive politics of mutual respect and inclusion.

The emphasis on citizenship may be a useful reminder to multiculturalists about what some of them may, at times, overlook, but it is not a critique or substitute for multiculturalism.

2. Critiques of Group Politics

This can take three forms:

a) Liberal societies can only recognise individual rights

While individual rights are fundamental to liberal democracies, much of social- democratic egalitarian politics would be impossible if we did not also recognise groups in various ways. For example, trades unions, in relation to collective bargaining; the Welsh language, as one of the national languages of Wales; the women's section in the Labour Party; positive action in relation to under-represented racial groups in a workplace; state funding for faith schools; the exemption of turban-wearing Sikhs from motor-cycle helmet safety laws.

These examples could be multiplied, and they suggest that a liberal democratic polity undertakes, in many different ways, to recognise and empower diverse kinds of groups.

b) Groups such as Muslims are internally diverse

There is an argument from social theory that groups are composed of individuals; there are no essential group characteristics, and no group monism, and so to talk about groups is theoretically facile, and usually masks a political motive.

It is true that we can sometimes work with crude ideas of groups, but that is not the same as saying that the groups that multiculturalists speak of do not exist. We do, perhaps, need looser concepts of groups, but the issue is to do with the nature of social categories, not multiculturalism *per se* (Modood, 2007, chapter 5). In this sense, all group categories are socially constructed, but it is clear that people do have a sense of groups (to which they feel they belong, or from which they are excluded).

One of the reasons we cannot ignore the communitarian conceptions of difference is that minorities often see and describe themselves as sharing a group identity through such categories as 'Jewish', 'Muslim' or 'Sikh', among others. If we accept that these are no less valid than categories of 'working-class', 'woman', 'black' or 'youth', it appears inconsistent to reject some groupist categories simply because they are subject to the same dialectical tension between specificity and generality that all group categories are subject to. This is not to 'essentialise' or 'reify', however, since the category of 'Jew', 'Muslim' or 'Sikh' can remain as internally diverse as 'Christian', 'Belgian' or 'middle-class', or any other category helpful in ordering our understanding.

c) **Hybridity and beyond race/ethnicity to multiple identities**
The above directly relates to the third point, namely that communal ethnicities are dissolving in front of our eyes, as people, especially young people, interact, mix, borrow, synthesise, and so on. It's not communities that people belong to, but an urban melange, alive to globalised and commercialised forms of recreation. Indeed, this is often what people are thinking of when they say that they like 'diversity', or are in favour of a multicultural society (but not multiculturalism).

Much research supports this sociological reading. But research also shows that such 'new ethnicities' and hybridities exist alongside, rather than simply replace, more prioritised identities (Modood *et al*, 1997; Modood, 1998). Just because we all have multiple identities does not mean that they are all equally important to us. Indeed, marginalised, stigmatised groups, groups that feel that they are always being talked about, stereotyped or are under political pressure – exactly the kind of minorities of concern to multiculturalism – are likely to be much more wedded to, if not one, a few identity elements, than to luxuriate in multiplicity.

This is exactly what we find with groups such as British Muslims, who are more likely to think that it is important to them that they are 'Muslim' and 'British' (typically both), and that these identities have a macro-significance that is present in most public contexts.

3. Secularism
Multiculturalism was not conceived in relation to religious groups, but groups championed by multiculturalists as racial or ethnic groups have

also started asserting, and sometimes giving primacy to, religious identities. This, then, causes friction or worse with those, including many multiculturalists, who assume that religion should be a private, not a public, even less a political, and certainly not a state, matter. From the other side, this looks just like an arbitrary, if historically grounded, bias against one kind of minority.

So, this has divided multiculturalists and weakened support for multi-culturalism. And the issue is not a minor matter, given the political salience of Muslims, and the estimate – only estimates are available – that they may form about 10 per cent or more of the population of western Europe by mid-century, with three times that proportion in the major cities, in some of which Muslims may be a majority.

But secularism is not, in all forms, inherently opposed to an ethno-religious communitarian multiculturalism. As a radical, ideological idea, it looks like that, and this is the favoured interpretation in France. But, as explained in chapter 2 and discussed further in chapter 11, in most democracies, secularism takes more moderate forms, and compromises between organised religion and the state are the norm. These compromises vary from country to country. For example, in the UK, bishops sit in the legislature, and religion is absent in electoral competitions; in the US, it's the other way round, but both countries are secular polities.

This means that, in every democratic secular polity, there are precedents, status quo arrangements, and institutional resources for accommodating some public claims of religious groups. I would suggest, therefore, that multiculturalists have to study these historical arrangements (for example, state funding of faith schools in England), and look to see how they can be multiculturalised, in other words used to meet the needs of new groups of citizens.

Sometimes the extension of a precedent will be regarded as controversial (for example, extending the legal recognition of Jewish courts of arbitration on matters such as divorce (the Beth Din) to Muslim ones), and sometimes faiths relatively new to Britain may raise issues without clear precedent. So, my point is not that there will be no political dilemmas in this area, but that there is no reason to exceptionalise and overproblematise the claims of religious groups by deceiving ourselves into thinking that they are incompatible with secularism.

Conclusion

My conclusion, then, is that many genuine criticisms of multicultura-lism have to be taken seriously, but none of them are reasons for aban-doning, rather than strengthening through modifying multiculturalism. In particular, that the three alleged challenges are actually akin to the qualifying ideas in that they are correctives not alternatives. I am sym-pathetic to all three challenges when they are combined with multi-culturalism, and used to correct, strengthen and go beyond each other. This is what I believe we tried to do in the CMEB (*cf* the quote at the head of this paper) and what I have tried to do (Modood, 2007).

It is a difficult and unstable combination, but I continue to think it is the task of the moment. What we need is a vision of citizenship that is not confined to the state, but dispersed across society, compatible with the multiple forms of contemporary groupness, and sustained through dia-logue; plural forms of representation that do not take one group as the model to which all others have to conform; and new, reformed national identities. That is multiculturalism.

Note

1 From: *Public Policy Research*, June – August, 2008, pp. 84-88, with permission from John Wiley and Sons; originally written for Multiculturalism: bringing us together or driving us apart? Round table held jointly by The Institute for Jewish Policy Research and The Runnymede Trust, 31 March 2008.

11

Moderate Secularism and Respect for Religion

Adapted from *Political Quarterly*, January 2010[1]

One of the features of the 'cultural turn' in social studies and of identity politics is that, while many think one or both may have gone too far, it is now commonplace that the classical liberal separation of culture and politics or the positivist-materialist distinctions between social structure and culture are mistaken. Yet religion – usually considered by social scientists to be an aspect of culture – continues to be uniquely held by some to be an aspect of social life that must be kept separate from at least the state, maybe from politics in general and perhaps even from public affairs at large, including the conversations that citizens have amongst themselves about their society. This religion-politics separationist view, which is clearly normative rather than scientific, can take quite different forms, either as an idea or as practice and can be more or less restrictive, I shall call 'secularism'. While acknowledging the variety of forms it can take I want to argue that one of the most important distinctions we need to make is between moderate and radical secularism. The failure to make this distinction is not just bad theory or bad social science but can lead to prejudicial, intolerant and exclusionary politics. I am particularly concerned with the prejudice and exclusion in relation to recently settled Muslims in Britain and the rest of western Europe but the points I wish to make have much more general application.

In the following I argue firstly at an abstract level that it is not necessary to insist on absolute separation, though of course it's a possible interpretation of secularism. Secondly I maintain that radical separation does not make sense in terms of historical actuality and contemporary adjustments. Thirdly, given that secularism does not necessarily mean the absence of state-religion connections, I would like to make a case for respect for religion as one of the values that citizens and a democratic state may choose to endorse. This may be a limiting case for secularism but is I think consistent with the norms and goals of a secular polity.

Radical and Moderate Secularism

If secularism is a doctrine of separation then we need to distinguish between modes of separation. Two modes of activity are separate when they have no connection with each other (absolute separation); but activities can still be distinct from each other even though there may be points of overlap (relative separation). The person who denies politics and religion are absolutely separate can still allow for relative separation. For example, in contemporary Islam there are ideological arguments for the absolute subordination of politics to religious leaders, as say propounded by the Ayatollah Khomeni in his concept of the *vilayat-i-faqih* (rule by religious scholar), but this is not mainstream Islam. Historically, Islam has been given a certain official status and preeminence in states in which Muslims ruled (just as Christianity or a particular Christian denomination had preeminence where Christians ruled). In these states Islam was the basis of state ceremonials and insignia, and public hostility against Islam was a punishable offence (sometimes a capital offence). Islam was the basis of jurisprudence but usually not directly of positive law. The state – legislation, decrees, law enforcement, taxation, military power, foreign policy, and so on – were all regarded as the prerogative of the ruler(s), of political power, which was regarded as having its own imperatives, skills, etc., and was rarely held by saints or spiritual leaders. Moreover, rulers had a duty to protect minorities. Similarly, while there have been Christians who have believed in or practiced theocratic rule (eg Calvin in Geneva) this is not mainstream Christianity, at least not for some centuries.

Just as it is possible to distinguish between theocracy and mainstream Islam, and theocracy and modern Christianity, so it is possible to distinguish between radical or ideological secularism, which argues for an absolute separation between state and religion, and the moderate forms that exist where secularism has become the order of the day, particularly Western Europe, with the partial exception of France. In nearly all of Western Europe there are points of symbolic, institutional, policy, and fiscal linkages between the state and aspects of Christianity. Secularism has increasingly grown in power and scope, but a historically evolved and evolving compromise with religion is the defining feature of Western European secularism, rather than the absolute separation of religion and politics. Secularism does today enjoy a hegemony in Western Europe, but it is a moderate rather than a radical, a pragmatic rather than an ideological, secularism.

Is There a Mainstream Western Secularism?

Having established at an abstract level that the mutual autonomy of religion and politics does not require their separation I would like to take further the point that while separation of religion and state/politics is a possible interpretation of secularism, it does not make sense in terms of historical actuality and contemporary adjustments. Rajeev Bhargava argues that 'in a secular state, a formal or legal union or alliance between state and religion is impermissible' and that 'for mainstream western secularism, separation means mutual exclusion' (Bhargava, 2008:88 and 103 respectively). What does he mean by 'mainstream western secularism'? His argument is that the secularism in the West has best developed in the United States and France, albeit in different ways. Americans have given primacy to religious liberty, and the French to equality of citizenship but in their differing ways they have come up with the best thinking on secularism that the West has to offer. 'These are the liberal and republican conceptions of secularism. Since these are the most dominant and defensible western versions of secularism, I shall put them together and henceforth designate them as the mainstream conception of secularism' (Bhargava, 2008). He is critical of this conception of western secularism which understands secularism in terms of separation and 'mutual exclusion'; this is common ground between us and so in my terms he is a 'moderate' not a 'radical' secularist. He has principled arguments about the nature of secularism and believes that the Indian polity today better exemplifies them than any western polity.

My concern here is with his characterisation of western secularism. I believe he is mistaken in arguing that the US and France are the best that the West had got to offer; and nor are they the dominant/mainstream conceptions. His argument is based on a poor understanding of the British experience and of the western European experience more generally. Most of western, especially north-western Europe, where France is the exception not the rule, is best understood in more evolutionary and moderate terms than Bhargava's characterisation of western secularism. They have several important features to do with a more pragmatic politics; with a sense of history, tradition and identity; and, most importantly, there is an accommodative character which is an essential feature of some historical and contemporary secularisms *in practice*. It is true that some political theorists and radical secularists have a strong tendency to abstract that out when talking about models and principles of secularism. If this tendency can be countered, British and other European experience ceases to be an inferior, non-mainstream instance of secularism but becomes mainstream and politically and normatively significant, if not superior to other versions.

Accommodative or moderate secularism, no less than liberal and republican secularism, can be justified in liberal, egalitarian, democratic terms, and in relation to a conception of citizenship. Yet it has developed a historical practice in which, explicitly or implicitly, organised religion is treated as a potential *public good* or *national resource* (not just a private benefit), which the state can in some circumstances assist to realise. This can take not only the form of an input into a legislative forum, such as the House of Lords, on moral and welfare issues; but also to being social partners to the state in the delivery of education, health and care services; to building social capital; or to churches belonging to 'the people'. So, that even those who do not attend them, or even sign up to their doctrines, feel they have a right to use them for weddings and funerals. All this is part of the meaning of what secularism means in most west European countries and it is quite clear that it is often lost in the models of secularism deployed by some normative theorists and public intellectuals. This is clearer today partly because of the development of our thinking in relation to the challenge of multicultural equality and the accommodation of Muslims, which highlight the limitations of the privatisation conception of liberal equality, and which sharpen the distinction between moderate/inclusive secularism and radical/ideological secularism. I have in my work expressly related the accommodative spirit of moderate secularism to the contemporary demands of multiculturalism (Modood, 2007).

I would argue that it is quite possible in a country like Britain to treat the claims of all religions in accordance with multicultural equality without having to abolish the established status of the Church of England, given that it has come to be a very 'weak' form of establishment and the Church has come to play a positive ecumenical and multi-faith role. Faced with an emergent multi-faith situation or where there is political will to incorporate previously marginalised faiths and sects and to challenge the privileged status of some religions the context-sensitive and conservationist response may be to pluralise the state-religion link rather than sever it. This indeed is happening across many countries in western Europe, despite critics on both the Left and the Right, especially among the radical secularists and the Islamophobic populists. In relation to the British case one can see this pluralising or multiculturalising in a number of incremental, ad hoc and experimental steps. For example, some years ago Prince Charles, the heir to the throne and to the office of Supreme Governor of the Church of England let it be known he would as monarch prefer the title 'Defender of Faith' to the historic title 'Defender of *the* Faith'. More recently, in 2004 the Queen used her Christmas television and radio broadcast – an important national occasion, especially for the older generation, on the most important Christian day of the year – to affirm the religious diversity of Britain. Her message was, in the words of Grace Davie:

> religious diversity is something which enriches society; it should be seen as a strength, not a threat; the broadcast moreover was accompanied by shots of the Queen visiting a Sikh temple and a Muslim centre. It is important to put these remarks in context. The affirmation of diversity as such is not a new idea in British society; what is new is the gradual recognition that religious differences should be foregrounded in such affirmations. Paradoxically, a bastion of privilege such as the monarchy turns out to be a key and very positive opinion former in this particular debate'. (Davie, 2007:232-33)

If such examples are regarded as merely symbolic then one should note how British governments have felt the need to create multi-faith consultative bodies. The Conservatives created an Inner Cities Religious Council in 1992, chaired by a junior minister, which was replaced by New Labour in 2006 with a body with a much broader remit, the Faith Communities Consultative Council. Moreover, the new Department of Communities and Local Government, which is represented in the Cabinet, has a division devoted to faith communities. This suggests that a 'weak establishment' or a reformed establishment can be one way of institutionalising religious pluralism. I am not suggesting it is the only or best way but in certain historical and political circumstances, it may indeed be a good way: we should be wary of ruling it out by arguments that appeal to 'the dominant and defensible western versions of secularism' (Bhargava, 2008:93). Stronger still: such institutional accommodation of minority or marginal faiths run with the grain of mainstream western European historic practice.

There can be many practical reasons that state policy may support religious groups (eg partnership in the delivery of healthcare); here I would tentatively like to suggest a reason that is not merely practical.

Respect for Religion

There is an image of religion as organisations or communities around competing truths, which are mutually intolerant, which perhaps even hate each other's guts. There is some truth in that in some times and places but the opposite is more important. Let me illustrate this by reference to my late father's, a devout and pious Muslim, decision that I should attend the daily Christian non-denominational worship at my secondary school. When I told him that I could be exempted from it, like the Jewish children, if he sent in a letter requesting this, he asked what they did during this time each morning. When I told him that some read comics, some took the opportunity to catch up with homework and some even arrived late, he said I should join the assembly. He said that as Christians mainly believe what we believe I should join in fully but whenever it was said that Jesus was the Son of God, I should say to myself, 'no, he is not'. It is a view that can perhaps be expressed as it is better to be in the presence of religion than not and so the value of religion does not simply reside in one's own religion. One's own religious heritage is to be cherished and honoured but so are those of others and the closing down of any religion is a loss of some sort.

I would suggest that historically it has been a prevalent view in the Middle East and South Asia, indeed where respect for the religion of others has extended to joining in the religious celebrations of others, borrowing from others, syncretism and so on. Respect for religion does not however require syncretism and can be found amongst contemporary Muslims in the West. Reporting on a recent Gallup World Poll, Dalia Mogahed and Zsolt Nyiri write of Muslims in Paris and London that their 'expectations of respect for Islam and its symbols extends to an expectation of respect for religion in general' and add that recently 'Shahid Malik, a British Muslim MP, even complained about what he called the 'policy wonks' who wished to strip the public sphere of all Christian religious symbols" (Mogahed and Niyiri, 2007:2). Some find this inter-faith fraternal spirit odd. After all, each religion claims to be true, and so why should it instil a respect for those of rival faiths? Well, if religion is about truth, which as we have seen is but one aspect of the meaning and value of a religion, then perhaps it approximates to a scientific community. Scientists can be highly competitive and determined to prove each other wrong – and yet such scientists evince intellectual appreciation and admiration for their rivals and researchers cooperate as well as compete.

Respect for religion is, clearly, above and beyond toleration. But also this valuing of religion and respect for the religion of others, even while not requiring participation, is based on a sense that religion is a good in itself, is a fundamental good and part of our humanity at a personal, social and civilisational level: it is an ethical good and so to be respected as a feature of human character just as we might respect truth-seeking, the cultivation of the intellect or the imagination or artistic creativity or self-discipline not just because of its utility or truth. We can think of religion as a good of this sort regardless of whether one is a believer or not, just as we can think music or science a good whether I am musical or scientific or not. A person, a society, a culture, or a country would be poorer without it. It is part of good living and while not all can cultivate it fully, it is good that some do and they should be honoured and supported by others.

This view is not dependent upon any kind of theism, for it can be a feature of some form of ethical humanism. I think it can be justified within a philosophy of human plurality and multi-dimensionality of the kind to be found in, for example, Collingwoood (1924) or Oakeshott (1933).

Respect for religion is, however, clearly more than respect as recognition or recognition of religious minorities and, while I am mainly concerned to argue for the latter, I am open to the former, especially as I believe that respect for religion is quite common amongst religious believers (the mirror-image of Dawkins) and I worry about an intolerant secularist hegemony. There may once have been a time in Europe when a powerful, authoritarian church or churches stifled dissent, individuality, free debate, science, pluralism and so on but that is not the present danger. Increasingly since the 1960s European cultural, intellectual and political life – the public sphere in the fullest sense of the word – has become dominated by secularism, with secularist networks and organisations controlling most of the levers of power., The accommodative character of secularism itself is being dismissed as archaic, especially on the centre-left. Thus respect for religion is made difficult and seems outlandish but may be necessary as one of the sources of counter-hegemony and a more genuine pluralism. Hence, respect for religion is compatible with and may be a requirement of a democratic political culture.

I appreciate that this may seem to be, and indeed may be a form of 'privileging' religion. For in this idea that the state may wish to show respect for religion I am going beyond not just toleration and freedom of religion but also beyond civic recognition. Nor am I simply pointing to the existence of overlaps and linkages between the state and religion. The sense of 'privilege' may not however be as strong as it may seem. After all, the autonomy of politics is the privileging of the non-religious, so this is perhaps qualifying that non-secular privileging. Moreover, it is far from an exclusive privileging. States regularly 'privilege' the nation, ethnicity, science, the arts, sport, economy and so on in relation to the centrality they give it in policy-making, the public resources devoted to it or the prestige placed upon it. So, if showing respect for religion is a privileging of religion, it is of a multiplex, multilogical sort; and it is based on the recognition that the secular is already dominant in many contemporary states.

Renewal of Christian and radical secular identities

Having pointed to a ground of optimism in relation to a multi-faith and multiculturalist society, let me conclude by pointing to some contemporary counter-trends. One of the themes of this book is the considerable negative reaction to Muslims. While in the main this is to do with a racialisation of Muslims in terms of culture, politics and terrorism, it is also manifested in relation to religion, secularism and the institutional accommodation of Muslims. Several trends can be identified. An example of an institutional accommodation resulting from Muslim pressure is that the 2001 UK Census included a religion question for the first time in its one hundred and fifty years' history; it was also exceptional in being a voluntary question, unlike the rest of the census form. Despite misgivings that the question would be declined, ninety-four per cent answered it. The real surprise, however, was the number of people who ticked themselves as 'Christian' (rather than 'no religion'). It was considerably higher than recorded in most surveys. For example, while in the British Social Attitudes survey of 1992, 31 per cent did not profess a belief in god(s) and in the latest BSA survey 43 per cent self-identified as non-religious (indeed 59 per cent did not describe themselves as religious) (Park *et al*, 2010), in the 2001 Census 72 per cent identified themselves as Christians and less than 16 per cent as without a religion.

While there is no one explanation for these variations, it is quite possible that the presence and salience of Muslims is stimulating a Christian identity. Voas and Bruce (2004) found that in neighbourhoods with high Muslim populations, the percentage of white Britons who chose 'Christian' is considerably higher than in similar, less mixed, neighbourhoods, even after controlling for various factors such as income. The emergence of a new, sometimes politically assertive cultural identification with Christianity has been noted in Denmark, and perhaps also in Germany.[2] It was politically apparent in the EU Constitution debate as well as in the ongoing debate about Turkey as a future EU member (Casanova, 2009). Some of the exponents of the former wanted a declaration to include a reference to Christianity as the religion of Europe. Even some of those who did not favour this openly reject Turkey as a possible EU member because it is not a Christian country and, worse, would bring a massive 70 millions Muslims into the EU.

These assertions of Christianity are not necessarily accompanied by any increase in expressions of faith or church attendance, which continue to decline across Europe. Giscard d'Estang, the former president of France, who who chaired the Convention on the Future of Europe, the body which drafted the (abortive) EU Constitution, expresses nicely the assertiveness I speak of: 'I never go to Church, but Europe is a Christian continent.' It has to be said, however, the political views about Europe referred to are held not just by cultural Christian identarians but also by many practising Christians, including the Catholic Church. It has been argued that Pope John Paul II 'looked at the essential cleavage in the world as being between religion and unbelief. Devout Christians, Muslims, and Buddhists had more in common with each other than with atheists' (Caldwell, 2009:151). Pope Benedict XVI, the same author contends, 'thinks that, within societies, believers and unbelievers exist in symbiosis. Secular westerners, he implies, have a lot in common with their religious fellows' (Caldwell, 2009: 151). The suggestion is that secularists and Christians in Europe have more in common with each other than they do with Muslims. That many secularists do not share Pope Benedict's view is evident from the fact that the proposed clause about Christianity was absent from the draft of the EU Constitution.[3] While there is little sign of a Christian Right in Europe of the kind that is strong in the US, there is to some degree a reinforcing or renewing of a sense that Europe is 'secular Christian', analogous to the term, 'secular Jew' to describe someone of Jewish descent who has a sense of Jewish identity but is not religiously practising and may even be an atheist.

Besides this secular Christian identity assertiveness which is to be found on the centre-right, though not exclusively, there is also a more radical secularism which is more characteristic of the left. It is a tradition that goes back to the Enlightenment (though more the French rather than the Scottish, English or German Enlightenment) and is not only non-religious but is often anti-religion. It has been most epigrammatically captured by Karl Marx's famous 'religion is the opium of the masses' and Nietzsche's 'God is dead'. Post-9/11 has seen the emergence of a radical discourse referred to as 'the new atheism' (Beattie, 2008; she has authors such as Richard Dawkins, Christopher Hitchens and Sam Harris in mind). Its political manifestation is found amongst intellectuals and political commentators such A.C. Grayling, Kenan

Malik and Polly Toynbee, organisations such as the National Secular Society and the British Humanist Association. They interpret political secularism to mean that religious beliefs and discourse should be excluded from the public sphere and/or politics and certainly activities endorsed or funded by the state. Thus they argue, for example, for the disestablishment of the Church of England, the removal of the Anglican bishops from the House of Lords and the withdrawal of state support for faith schools (the greatest beneficiary of which in terms of secondary schooling is the Catholic church). With groups like Muslims, Sikhs and Hindus pressing to have some of these benefits extended to themselves (as to some extent has already happened in the case of the Jews) and religious groups more involved in the delivery of welfare and urban renewal, it is clear that this radical political secularism is not only a break with the inherited *status quo* secularism in most parts of Western Europe (with France being something of an exception) but is at odds with the current institutionalisation of religious pluralism.

Which of these will become dominant, or how these trends may develop, interact and synthesise is not clear. The critical issue of principle is not how but *whether* religious groups, especially those that are marginal and under-represented in public life, ought to be represented. The real problem today, however, is with an approach that eschews difference-blindness in general but would not dream of being anything other than religion-blind. Take the BBC – an organisation with a deserved reputation for public service and high standards, an aspect of which is manifested in the remark by a serving Director-General, Greg Dykes, that the organisation was 'hideously white' (Dykes, 2002). Relatedly, for some years now it has given political importance to reviewing and improving its personnel practices and its output of programmes, including its on-screen 'representation' of the British population, by making provision for and winning the confidence of women, ethnic minority groups and young people. Why should it not also use religious groups as a criterion of inclusivity and have to demonstrate that it is doing the same for viewers and staff defined by religious community membership?

Nevertheless, despite initial governmental reluctance, measures in the new Equalities Act (2010) to address religious discrimination have been scaled up to match those of other unlawful forms of discrimination.

There is, though, no prospect at present of religious equality catching up with the importance that employers and other organisations give to sex or race in the UK (outside Northern Ireland). This is partly related to the European historical experience of religion as a source of prejudice and conflict, a memory which has been reactivated by the presence of militant Muslims, not to mention networks of terrorists. It is a matter of concern that this fear of Muslims is strengthening intolerant, exclusionary politics across Europe. Specifically, it is one of the arguments of this book that the fact that some people are today developing cultural Christianity and/or secularism as an ideology to oppose Islam and its public recognition is a challenge both to pluralism and equality, and thus to some of the bases of contemporary democracy. This is not just a risk to democracy as such but, in the present context of high levels of fear of and hostility to Muslims and Islam, threatens to create a long term racialised-religious division in Europe.

Notes

1 Based on a part of and developed out of my 'Moderate Secularism, Religion as Identity and Respect for Religion', *Political Quarterly*, January, 2010, Vol 81 (1), 4-14, with kind permission of John Wiley and Sons.

2 In the general election of 2010, Nick Griffin, the leader of the BNP used a 'Christian nation' rhetoric, saying, 'I'm an Anglican. By blood, by descent, by the way I was brought up, by my schooling and so on' (Bartley, 2010a). Interestingly, he makes no reference to beliefs or values. Nevertheless, the new Christian Party, which is clearly based on an understanding of Christianity, endorsed the stand of the BNP on immigration (Bartley, 2010b).

3 Which was not ratified by the Council of Ministers and so was missing from the final document and the Lisbon Treaty.

Bibliography

Ahmed, AS (2003) *Islam Under Siege*. Oxford: Polity

Ahmed, L (1992) *Women and Gender in Islam: Historical Roots of a Modern Debate*. New Haven, Connecticut: Yale University Press

Akhtar, S (1989) *Be Careful With Muhammud*. London: Bellew Publishing

Alavi, H (1987) Pakistan and Islam: Ethnicity and Ideology. In Halliday, F and Alavi, H (eds) *State and Ideology in the Middle East and Pakistan*. London: Macmillan

Alibhai, Y (1989) Home Truths. *Observer* (Colour Supplement), 10 November 1989 p46-49

Ameli SR (2002) *Globalization, Americanization and British Muslim Identity*. London: ICAS Press

Anwar, M (1984) Employment Patterns of Muslims in Western Europe. *Journal of Muslim Minority Affairs* 1

Anwar, M (1986) *Young Muslims in a Multi-Cultural Society*. Leicester: The Islamic Foundation

Asad, T (2003) *Formations of the Secular*. California: Stanford University Press

Asani, AS (2003) 'So That You May Know One Another": A Muslim American Reflects on Pluralism and Islam. *The Annals of the American Academy of Political and Social Sciences* 588 p40-51. Islam: Enduring Myths and Changing Realities, Special Editor: Aslam Syed

Back, L (1993) Race, Identity and Nation within an Adolescent Community in South London. *New Community* 19(2) p217-233

Badawi, MAZ (2003) Citizenship in Islam. *Association of Muslim Social Scientists (UK) Newsletter 6* p17-20

Baksh, N (2005) Waking up to Progressive Muslims. *Q-News* 361, March 2005

Bari, A (2005) *Race, Religion and Multiculturalism*. London: Renaissance Press

Barry, B (2001) *Culture Equality*. Cambridge: Polity Press

Bartley, J (2010a) Nick Griffin Expresses Support for Sentamu and Nazir Ali. *Ekklesia*, 24 March 2010 http://ekklesia.co.uk/node/11599 (Last visited May 2010)

Bartley, J (2010b) Christian Party Endorses BNP Stance on Immigration from the EU. *Ekklesia*, 24 March 2010 http://ekklesia.co.uk/node/11598 (Last visited May 2010)

BBC (2005) Blair Shuns US Religion Politics. *BBC News*, 22 March 2005 http://news.bbc.co.uk/1/hi/uk_politics/4369481.stm (Last visited May 2010)

Beattie, T (2008) *The New Atheists: The Twilight of Reason and the War on Religion.* New York: Orbis Books

Bechler, R (2004) A Bridge Across Fear: an Interview with Tariq Ramadan. *Open Democracy*, 13 July 2004 http://www.opendemocracy.net/faith-europe_islam/article_2006.jsp (Last visited May 2010)

Bhargava, R. (2008) Political Secularism. In Levey, G and Modood, T (eds) *Secularism, Religion and Multicultural Citizenship.* Cambridge: Cambridge University Press

Binder, L (1986) Islam, Ethnicity and the State in Pakistan: An Overview. In Hanauzizi, A and Weiner, M (eds) *The State, Religion and Ethnic Politics, Afghanistan, Iran and Pakistan.* Syracuse: Syracuse University Press

Bokhari, K (2004) Who are 'Moderate' Muslims? *Q-News*, March 2004

Bonnett, A (1993) *Radicalism, Anti-Racism and Representation.* London; New York: Routledge

Brohi, A (1979) Mawlana Abul Ala Mawdudi: the Man, the Scholar, the Reformer. In Ahmad, K and Ansari, Z (eds) *Islamic Perspectives.* Leicester: The Islamic Foundation

Caldwell, C. (2009) *Reflections on the Revolution in Europe*, London: Penguin Books

Carens, J (2000) *Culture, Citizenship and Community: A Contextual Exploration of Justice as Evenhandedness.* Oxford: Oxford University Press

Casanova, J (2009) Immigration and the New Religious Pluralism: a European Union – United States Comparison. In Levey, G and Modood, T (eds) *Secularism, Religion and Multicultural Citizenship.* Cambridge: Cambridge University Press

Castells, M (1997) *The Information Age: Economy, Society and Culture Volume II: The Power of Identity.* Oxford: Blackwell Publishers

Cohen, P (1988) The Perversions of Inheritance: Studies in the Making of Multi-racist Britain. In Cohen, P and Bains, HS (eds) *Multi-Racist Britain.* London: Macmillan

Collingwood RG (1924) *Speculum Mentis.* Oxford: Oxford University Press

CMEB (Commission on Multi-Ethnic Britain) (2000) *The Future of Multi-Ethnic Britain* (the Parekh Report). London: Profile Books

Connor, H, Tyers, C, Modood, T and Hillage, J (2004) *Why the Difference?: A Closer Look at Higher Education Minority Ethnic Students and Graduates.* DfES Research Report RR552 www.dfes.gov.uk/research/data/uploadfiles/RB552.pdf (Last visited May 2010)

Daily Express (1989) Race Survey Shock, 30 August 1989

Daniel, N (1961) *Islam and the West Vol. 1, Making of an Image, 1000-1300 A.D.* Edinburgh: Edinburgh University Press

Daniel, N. (1967) *Islam and the West Vol. 2, Islam, Europe and Empire.* Edinburgh: Edinburgh University Press

Davie, G (2007) Pluralism, Tolerance, and Democracy: Theory and Practice in Europe. In Banchoff, T (ed) *Democracy and the New Religious Pluralism*. New York: Oxford University Press

Dykes, G (2002) Diversity in Broadcasting: a Public Service Perspective. *BBC Press Office*, 3 May 2002 http://www.bbc.co.uk/pressoffice/speeches/stories/dyke_cba. shtml (Last visited May 2010)

Fouché, G (2006) Danish Paper Rejected Jesus Cartoons. *The Guardian*, 6 February 2006

Gittoes, M and Thompson, J (2007) Admissions to Higher Education: Are there Biases Against or in Favour of Ethnic Minorities? *Teaching in Higher Education* 12(3) p419 – 424

Gove, M (2006) *Celsius 7/7*. London: Weidenfeld and Nicolson

Hamburger, P (2002) *Separation of Church and State*. Cambridge, Massachusetts: Harvard University Press

Hayes, D (2005) What Kind of Country? *OpenDemocracy*, 28 July 2005 http://www. opendemocracy.net/conflict-terrorism/britain_2713.jsp (Last visited May 2010)

Held, D (1995) *Democracy and the Global Order: From the Modern State to Cosmopolitan Governance*. Stanford: Stanford University Press

Hobohm, M (1978) Islam and the Racial Problem. In Gauhar, A (ed) *The Challenge of Islam*. London: Islamic Council of Europe

Impact International (1989) The Long March Against Sacrilege, 22 June 1989 p10-12

Jacobson, J (1997) Religion and Ethnicity: Dual and Alternative Sources of Identity among Young British Pakistanis. *Ethnic and Racial Studies* 20 (2) p238-256

Jacobson, DA (1997) *Rights Across Borders: Immigration and the Decline of Citizenship*. Baltimore: Johns Hopkins University Press

Johnson, R (1989) Wars of Religion. *New Statesman and Society*, 15 December 1989

Keppel, G (2005) Europe's Answer to Londonistan. *OpenDemocracy*, 23 August http:// www.opendemocracy.net/conflict-terrorism/londonistan_2775.jsp# (Last visited May 2010)

Khan, MAM (2002) *American Muslims: Bridging Faith and Freedom*. Beltsville, Maryland: Amana Publications

Kymlicka, W (1992) Two Models of Pluralism and Tolerance. *Analyse and Kritik, Zeitschrift für Sozialwissenschaften* 13 p33-56

Kymlicka, W (1995) *Multicultural Citizenship*. Oxford: Oxford University Press

Kymlicka, W (2001) *Politics in the Vernacular: Nationalism, Multiculturalism and Citizenship*. Oxford: Oxford University Press

Leonard, K (2003) American Muslim Politics: Discourses and Practices. *Ethnicities* 3(2) p147-181

Leonard, M (1997) *Britain: Renewing Our Identity*. London: Demos

Lewis, P (1994) *Islamic Britain: Religion, Politics and Identity among British Muslims*. London: I B Tauris

Malik, K (1989) Muslim Britain – A Community Provoked. *The Voice*, 30 May 1989 (originally in Living Marxism)

Mamdani, M (2002) Good Muslim, Bad Muslim: A Political Perspective on Culture and Terrorism. In Hershberg, E and Moore, KW (eds) *Critical Views of September 11*. New York: The New Press.

Mawdudi, A (1976) *Human Rights in Islam*. Leicester: The Islamic Foundation

Mawdudi, A (1986) *The Islamic Way of Life*. (Ahmad, K and Murad, K (eds)). Leicester: The Islamic Foundation

Meer, N, Dwyer, C and Modood, T (2010) 'Embodying Nationhood? Conceptions of British National Identity, Citizenship and Gender in the 'Veil Affair'. *The Sociological Review*, 58(1):84-111

Meer, N and Modood, T (2009) The Multicultural State We Are In: Muslims, 'Multi-culture' and the 'Civic re-balancing' of British Multiculturalism. *Political Studies* 57(3) p473-497

Meer, N and Noorani, T (2008) A Comparison of Anti-Semitism and Anti-Muslim Sentiment in Britain. *Sociological Review* 56(2) p195-219

Mernissi, F (1991) *Women and Islam: An Historical and Theological Enquiry*. (translated by Lakeland, M J). Oxford: Basil Blackwell

Miles, R (1989) *Racism*. London; New York: Routledge

Modood, T (1988) 'Black', Racial Equality and Asian Identity. *New Community* 14 p397-404

Modood, T (1989) Religious Anger and Minority Rights. *Political Quarterly* 60(3) p280-284

Modood, T (1990) Colour, Class and Culture: the Three Cs of Race. *Equal Opportunities Review*, March 1990

Modood, T (1994) Muslim Identity: Social Reality or Political Project?. In Rex, J and Modood, T *Muslim Identity: Real or Imagined?* Centre for the Study of Islam and Christian-Muslim Relations Paper Europe No 12, University of Birmingham

Modood, T (1997) Introduction: The Politics of Multiculturalism in the New Europe. In Modood, T (2002) The Place of Muslims in British Secular Multiculturalism. In Alsayyad, N and Castells, M (eds) *Muslim Europe or Euro-Islam: Politics, Culture and Citizenship in the Age of Globalisation*. New York: Lexington Books (reproduced in Modood (2005))

Modood, T (1998) 'Anti-Essentialism, Multiculturalism and the 'Recognition' of Religious Minorities', *Critical Review of International, Social and Political Philosophy* 6(1) p378-399

Modood, T (2004) Capitals, Ethnic Identity and Educational Qualifications. *Cultural Trends* 13(2) No 50 p87-105

Modood, T (2005) *Multicultural Politics: Racism, Ethnicity and Muslims in Britain*. Minneapolis: University of Minnesota Press and Edinburgh: Edinburgh University Press

Modood, T (2007) *Multiculturalism: A Civic Idea*. Cambridge: Polity Press

Modood, T (2010) 'Moderate Secularism, Religion as Identity and Respect for Religion', *Political Quarterly*, 8(1) p4-14

Modood, T, Berthoud, R, Lakey, J, Nazroo, J, Smith, P, Virdee, S and Beishon, S (1997) *Ethnic Minorities in Britain: Diversity and Disadvantage*. London: Policy Studies Institute

Modood, T and May, S (2001) Multiculturalism and Education in Britain: An Internally Contested Debate. *International Journal of Educational Research* 35 p305-317.

Modood, T, Triandafyllidou, A and Zapata-Barrero, R (2006) (eds) *Multiculturalism, Muslims and Citizenship: A European Approach*. London: Routledge

Mogahed, D and Nyiri, Z (2007) Reinventing Integration: Muslims in the West. *Harvard International Review* 29(2) http://www.harvardir.org/articles/1619/ (Last visited May 2010)

Mouritsen, P (2006) The Particular Universalism of a Nordic Civic Nation. In Modood, T, Triandafyllidou, A and Zapata-Barrero, R (eds) *Multiculturalism, Muslims and Citizenship: A European Approach*. London; New York: Routledge

National Equality Panel (NEP) (2010) *An Anatomy of Economic Inequality in the UK*, London: Government Equalities Office

Murphy, D (1987) *Tales from Two Cities*. London: John Murray

Oakeshott MJ (1933) *Experience and its Modes*. Cambridge: Cambridge University Press

Parekh, B (1989) Between Holy Text and Moral Void. *New Statesman and Society*, 24 March 1989 p29-33

Parekh, B (2000) *Rethinking Multiculturalism: Cultural Diversity and Political Theory*. Basingstoke: Palgrave

Parekh, B (2003) Muslims in Britain. *Prospect* 88, 20 July 2003

Park, A, Curtice, J, Thomson, K, Phillips, M, Clery, E and Butt, S (2010) *British Social Attitudes: The 26th Report*. London: Sage Publications

Pffaff, W (2005) A Monster of Our Own Making. *Observer*, 21 August 2005 http://www.guardian.co.uk/alqaida/story/0,12469,1553504,00.html (Last visited May 2010)

Phillips, A (2007) *Multiculturalism Without Culture*. Princeton, NJ: Princeton University Press

Phillips, M (2006) *Londonistan*. London: Gibson Square.

Poulter, S (1986) *English Law and Ethnic Minority Customs*. London: Butterworths

Prins, G and Salisbury, R (2008) Risk, Threat and Security, the Case of the United Kingdom. *The RUSI Journal* (Royal United Services Institute) 153(1) p22-27

Rahman, F (1982) *Islam and Modernity*. Chicago: University of Chicago Press

Ramadan, T (2004a) *Western Muslims and the Future of Islam*. Oxford: Oxford University Press

Ramadan, T (2004b) An Oft-Repeated 'Truth'. *The Guardian*, 31 August 2004

Rex, J (1988) The Urban Sociology of Religion and Islam in Birmingham. In Gerholm, T and Lithman, Y (eds) *The New Islamic Presence in Western Europe.* London: Mansell

Rex, J and Jospehides, S (1987) Asian and Greek Cypriot Associations and Identity. In Rex, J, Joly, D and Wilpert, C (eds) *Immigrant Associations in Europe.* Aldershot: Gower

Robinson, F (1988) *Varieties of South Asian Islam.* Coventry: Centre for Research in Ethnic Relations

Roy, O (2004) *Globalised Islam: The Search for a New Ummah.* London: Hurst

Rushdie, S (1989) Choice Between Light and Dark. *Observer,* 22 January 1989

Sacks J (2007) *The Home We Build Together: Recreating Society.* London: Continuum

Safi, O (2003) (ed) *Progressive Muslims.* Oxford: One World

Sandel, M (1994) Review of Rawls' Political Liberalism. *Harvard Law Review* 107 p1765-1794

Sardar, Z (1987) *The Future of Muslim Civilisation* (Second Edition). London: Mansell

Sardar, Z (2002) Multiculturalism. In Sardar, Z *The A to Z of Postmodern Life.* London: Vision

Sardar, Z (2004) *Beyond Difference: Cultural Relations in the New Century.* Lecture for the British Council's 70th Anniversary. London: British Council

Sayyid, S (2003) Muslims in Britain: Towards A Political Agenda. In Seddon, MS, Hussain, D and Malik, N (eds) *British Muslims: Loyalty and Belonging,* Leicester: The Islamic Foundation and London: The Citizen Organising Foundation

Shadid, WAR and Van Koningsveld, PS (1996) Loyalty to a non-Muslim Government: An Analysis of Islamic Normative Discussions and of the Views of Some Contemporary Islamicists. In Shahid, WAR and Van Koningsveld, PS *Political Participation and Identities of Muslims in Non-Muslim States.* Kampen, The Netherlands: Kok Pharos Publishing House

Shah, B, Dwyer, C and Modood, T (forthcoming) 'Explaining Educational Achievement and Career Aspirations among Young British Pakistanis: Mobilising 'Ethnic Capital'. *Sociology*

Shaw, A (1988) *A Pakistani Community in Britain.* Oxford: Basil Blackwell

Shiner, M and Modood, T (2002) Help or Hindrance? Higher Education and the Route to Ethnic Equality. *British Journal of Sociology of Education* 23(2) p209-232

Smith, W (1957) *Islam in Modern History.* Princeton, NJ: Princeton University Press

Soysal, YN (1994) *Limits of Citizenship: Migrants and Postnational Membership in Europe.* Chicago; London: University of Chicago Press

Swann, M (1985) *Education for All.* Cmnd. 9453. London: HMSO

Taylor, C (1994) Multiculturalism and 'The Politics of Recognition'. In Gutmann, A (ed) Multiculturalism and '*The Politics of Recognition*'. Princeton: Princeton University Press

Troyna, B (1993) *Racism and Education*. Buckingham: Open University Press

Troyna, B (1987) (ed) *Racial Inequality in Education*. London: Tavistock

Uberoi, V and Modood, T (2010) 'Who Doesn't Feel British? Divisions Over Muslims'. *Parliamentary* Affairs 63(2) p302-320

UK Action Committee on Islamic Affairs (1989) *The British Muslim Response to Mr. Patten*

Vertovec, S (2006) *The Emergence of Super-Diversity in Britain*. Working Paper No. 5. Centre on Migration, Policy and Society (COMPAS): University of Oxford

Voas, D and Bruce, S (2004) Research Note: The 2001 Census and Christian Identification in Britain. *Journal of Contemporary Religion* 19(1) p23-28

Wadud, A (1999) *Qur'an and Woman: Rereading the Sacred Text from a Woman's Perspective*. New York: Oxford University Press

Werbner, P (2001) Divided Loyalties. *Times Higher Education Supplement,* 14 December 2001

Werbner, P (2002) *Imagined Diasporas Among Manchester Muslims*. Oxford: James Currey

Winter, T (2003) Muslim Loyalty and Belonging: Some Reflections on the Psychosocial Background. In Seddon, MS, Hussain, D and Malik, N (eds) *British Muslims: Loyalty and Belonging*. Leicester: The Islamic Foundation and London: The Citizen Organising Foundation

Wolf, M (2005) When Multiculturalism is a Nonsense. *Financial Times*, 31 August 2005 http://news.ft.com/cms/s/4c751acc-19bc-11da-804e-00000e2511c8.html (Last visited May 2010)

WAF (Women Against Fundamentalism) (1990) Founding Statement. *Women Against Fundamentalism* 1(1)

Wyn-Davies, M (1988) *Knowing One Another: Shaping An Islamic Anthropology*. London: Mansell

Young, IM (1990) *Justice and the Politics of Difference*. Princeton, NJ: Princeton University Press

Yuval-Davis, N (1992) Fundamentalism, Multiculturalism and Women in Britain. In Donald, J and Rattansi, A (eds) *Race, Culture and Difference*. London: Sage